CLEAR HABIT

# THE POWER OF HABITS

## YOU ARE ONE DECISION AWAY FROM UNBELIEVABLE SUCCESS IN LIFE

Wilson Smith

# Table of Contents

# PART 1

# Chapter 1:

# *What To Do When You Feel Like Your Work is not Good Enough*

Feeling like your work is not good enough is very common; your nerves can get better of you at any time throughout your professional life. There is nothing wrong with nerves; It tells you that you care about improving and doing well. Unfortunately, too much nervousness can lead to major self-doubt, and that can be crippling. You are probably very good at your work, and when even once you take a dip, you think that things are not like how they seem to you. If this is something you're feeling, then you're not alone, and this thing is known as Imposter Syndrome. This term is used to describe self-doubt and inadequacy. This one thing leaves people fearing that there might be someone who will expose them. The more pressure you apply to yourself, the more dislocation is likely to occur. You create more anxiety, which creates more fear, which creates more self-doubt. You don't have to continue like this. You can counter it.

**Beyond Work**

If your imposter syndrome affects you at work, you should take some time out and start focusing on other areas of your life. There are chances that there is something in your personal life that is hindering your work life. This could be anything your sleep routine, friends, diet, or even your relationships. There is a host of external factors that can affect your performance. If there are some boxes you aren't ticking, then there is a high chance of you not performing well at work.

## You're Better Than You Think

When you're being crippled by self-doubt, the first thing you have to think about is why you were hired in the first place. The interviewers saw something in you that they believed would improve the business.

So, do you think they would recruit someone who can't do the job? No, they saw your talent, they saw something in you, and you will come good.

When you find yourself in this position, take a moment to write down a few things that you believe led to you being in the role you are now. What did those recruiters see? What did your boss recognize in you? You can also look back on a period of time where you were clicking and felt victorious. What was different then versus now? Was there an external issue like diet, exercise, socializing, etc.?

Check Yourself Before You Wreck Yourself

A checklist might be of some use to you. If you have a list to measure yourself against, then it gives you more than just one thing to judge yourself against. We're far too quick to doubt ourselves and criticize harshly.

The most obvious checklist in terms of work is technical or hard skills, but soft skills matter, too. It's also important to remember that while you're technically proficient now, things move quickly, and you'll reach a point where everything changes, and you have to keep up. You might not ever excel at something, but you can accept the change and adapt to the best of your ability.

It matters that you're hard-working, loyal, honest, and trustworthy. There's more to judge yourself on than just your job. Even if you make a mistake, it's temporary, and you can fix it.

Do you take criticism well? Are you teachable? Easy to coach? Soft skills count for something, which you can look to even at your lowest point and recognize you have strengths.

When you're struggling through a day, week, or even a month, take one large step backward and think about what it is you're unhappy with. What's causing your unhappiness, and how can you improve it?

It comes down to how well you know yourself. If you're clear on what your values are and what you want out of life, then you're going to be fine. If the organization you work for can't respect your values and harness your strengths, then you're better off elsewhere. So, it is extremely important to take time out for that self check-in there could be times you talk to yourself in negative light. Checking in with yourself regularly and not feeding yourself negativity could be one-step forward.

# Chapter 2:

# <u>10 Habits of Happy People</u>

Happy people live the most satisfying lives on the planet. They have come to understand the importance of not worrying because it will not make any differential change in their lives. If you cannot control the outcome of a process, why worry? If you can control and make a difference to the outcome of a situation, why worry? Worrying does not bring an ounce of success your way.

Here are 10 habits of happy people that could be you if you choose to adopt it:

1.  <u>Happy People Count Their Blessings.</u>

Taking stock of your successes is an important part of appreciating yourself. You find comfort in knowing that despite all the hiccups you have found in your journey there remains an oasis of achievements in your desert.

Everyone needs to take stock of what is in his or her basket of blessings. It is a reminder of your resilience and persistence in the face of challenges. It is an indication of your ability and a minute representation of the progress you can make, given time.

Remind yourself of the taste of victory in your small achievements. It begins with understanding that you definitely cannot be able to win it all. There are grey and shadow areas that will not be within your reach.

## 2.  Happy People Do Not Need the Validation of Others.

Happy people do not wait for the validation of other people. They are autonomous. Develop the habit of doing what is right regardless of your audience and you will have an authentic lifestyle. As such, your source of happiness will be independent of uncontrollable factors. Why should you tie your happiness to someone else capable of ruining your day in a snap? This is not to mean that you will not need other people. Humans are social beings and interdependent. Letting them strongly influence your lifestyle is the major problem. Be your own man.

## 3.  They Are Bold.

Boldly and cautiously pursuing their ambitions is part of the ingredients that make up happy people. Knowing what you want is one thing and pursuing it is another. If music is your passion and it makes you happy, chase after it for it is therein that your happiness lies. Whatever it is (of course considering its legality) do not let it pass.

To be truly happy, do not live in the shadow of other happy people. Define your happiness and drink from your well. Timidity will make you bask under the shade of giants and create a sense of false security. One day the shade will be no more and leave you exposed to an unimaginable reality.

## 4.  They are social people.

Being social is one common characteristic of happy people. Happiness makes them bubbly and alive. There is a common testament in almost all happy people – either happiness made them social or their social nature made them happy. Thanks to whichever of the two came earlier, they are happy people!

Like bad luck, happiness is contagious. Your social circle can infect you with happiness or even deny it to you. Being sociable does not mean to the extreme nature with all the hype that comes along.

It means being approachable to people. Some will positively add to your basket and others will offer positive criticism towards your cause. With such input, your happiness will have longevity.

5.   Believe in a greater cause.

Happy people understand that it is not always about them. There is a greater cause above their interests. They do not derive their happiness from the satisfaction of their needs and wants. Regardless of any deficiency in their lives, their flame of happiness is not easily put out.

Do you want to be happy? It is time to put self-interest aside and not tie your happiness to local anchors. An average person's happiness is mainly dependent on his well-being. Refusing to be average gives you leverage over those out to put off your happiness.

6.   Lead a purposeful life.

Are there happy people without purpose? Those we see happy maintain their status by having a powerful drive towards the same. A strong purpose will make you stay on happiness' lane. It is the habit of happy people to have a purpose. This is to enable them to stay on course.

Being happy is not a permanent state. It is easily reversible if caution is not taken. Purposefulness is part of the caution taken by happy people.

### 7. Admit they are human.

To err is human. Given this, happy people appreciate the erroneous nature of man and accept the things they cannot change, have the courage to change the things they can, and the wisdom to know the difference. A prayer commonly referred to as the serenity prayer.

Admitting being human is the first step towards being happy. You forgive yourself of your wrongs before seeking the forgiveness of another. This brings inner peace culminating in happiness.

### 8. Know their strengths and weaknesses.

Being aware of your strengths and weaknesses is one thing happy people have mastered. Through that, they know their limits; the time to push and time to take a break. This serves to help avoid unwarranted disappointments that come along with new challenges.

Nothing can put off the charisma of a prepared spirit. Happy people know their limitations well enough such that no ill-willed voice can whisper disappointments to them. They hold the power of self-awareness within their hearts making them live with contentment.

### 9. Notice the contributions of those around them.

No man is an island. The contributions of other people in our lives cannot be emphasized enough. We are because they are (for all the good reasons). At any one point in our lives, someone made us happy. The first step is noticing the roles played by those in our immediate environment.

The joy of being surrounded by people to hold our hands in life is engraved deeper in our hearts in times of need. It is time you stop looking far away and turn your eyes to see what is next to you.

10. <u>They are grateful and appreciative.</u>

"Thank you" is a word that does not depart from the lips of happy people. Their hearts are trained to focus on what is at their disposal instead of what they cannot reach. It is crystal that a bird in hand is worth two in the bush.

Happy people continue being happy despite deficiencies. Try being appreciative and see how happiness will tow along.

Adopt these 10 habits of happy people and depression will keep away from you. If you want to be happy, do what happy people do and you will see the difference.

# Chapter 3:

## 8 Habits That Help You Live Longer

Habits define who you are. Each habit influences your life on a positive and negative dimensions. After all, smoking a cigarette is a habit, and so are long hours of jogging. The behaviors that negative you from attaining your full potential also shorten your life.

Exercising, consuming nutritious meals, meditating, among others, makes our lives better in immeasurable ways. Our habits take over as an autopilot when our physical and mental abilities ebb and flow with age. This is especially true if you are old enough to understand the importance of habits but still young enough to make your positive habits count. As you get older, you'll find yourself relying more and more on your habits. Create good habits, and they will serve as the autopilot on which you will trust to stay healthy, active, and engaged.

As you create and stick to that habit you love, keep longevity and quality life your ultimate goal. Even if you've had bad habits in the past, now is the moment to break them.

Here are 8 habits that could help you live a longer life.

## 1. Exercise Regularly.

Studies show that frequent, intense exercising is essential for age and physical health preservation. Getting out of your comfort zone to engage in a challenging exercise will reap benefits in the long haul. Hopping on a treadmill at a snail-like pace will do you no good. Therefore, it would help if you stalled rigorous aerobic exercises, stretching to your habit menu.

The less flexible you are, the more likely you will trip, break your hip, and end up in a nursing home like Aunt Karen. Vigorous exercise and stretching your body are the best ways to protect yourself from preventable injuries and the physical ailments of aging.

# 2. Mind Training

Mind training is equally vital as body exercises as you become older. As you train your body, your mind also needs activity to stay in good form. Learn and challenge yourself to remain alert and possibly avoid dementia. There are many mind training exercises such as puzzles, or even Sudoku, or any mind-challenging tasks.

According to a recent study conducted by John Hopkins Medicine, staying in school longer reduces the prevalence of dementia in the United States, particularly among individuals aged 65 and older.

# 3. Keep a Healthy Weight.

Maintaining a healthy body means that you are cautious of what you consume. Consider the foods that enhance your physical, mental and spiritual wellbeing by avoiding calories and refined food staff. A new article in Medical News Today by Catharine Paddock, Ph.D., advocates keeping your body mass index (BMI) under 25% if possible. Keep your body weight as healthy as possible! It will impact your longevity.

## 4. Develop a Positive Mental Attitude.

Whatever your viewpoint is on your present living conditions, impact your life in the long haul. That is, your take on your current life significantly reacts with the functioning of your body and soul. Therefore, people who adopt and adjust to a positive stereotype about aging are likely to recover faster from any disability. As a result, according to a recent study published in the Journal of the American Medical Association, longevity is achieved by maintaining positive thoughts towards your current state of affairs.

## 5. Elevate Your Mood.

As we become older, depression and anxiety might become more prevalent. Do anything you can to boost your mood, whether it's through exercise or exciting mental activity. Go for walks in the park, re-enter the dating scene, or volunteer for a cause you care about – in short, do anything that makes you feel better about yourself and the world.

## 6. Maintain Your Social Contacts.

Maintaining a social connection becomes meaningful as you grow older. You don't need a considerable social network; an influential network is enough. Your family, accordingly, may be enough, but only if the members are happy and flourishing. The Inverse is very true! If you find that your social network is exceptionally negative, look for ways to create a new one.

Make friends of different ages who may have other interests than you, and keep fostering friendships you already have or may have had in the past. Remember, that person you allow in your inner circle is equally important.

## 7. Take Charge of Your Life

Rather than being a spectator, own your life. Don't just sit and watch the world pass you. Just get out and about, engage in activities that matter at every stage of your life. This means doing what a 25 or 40-year-old does to avoid mid-life crises. It can be not easy, especially in today's internet era, where we can check what other people are up to at the hour without even leaving the couch. On the other hand, sitting on the sidelines will not help you maintain excellent physical or mental health. Make sure you're not only listening to other people's experiences; get out there and make your own.

## 8. Do Something Valuable.

Having a purpose in life and living up to it is vital. The drive doesn't have to be extravagant or mid-blowing to be meaningful as most of us think. Some people find their purpose in being an outstanding grandparent, volunteering for a cause important to them, or even mastering woodworking or gardening skills. It doesn't matter what your goal is as long as you have one.

On the other hand, not having a purpose might lead to poor habits that negatively impact your longevity and mood. Consider this: if you don't have anything to do, you can end up sitting in front of the TV all day, or worse, falling into the meaningless emptiness of social media.

## Conclusion

The great news is that you don't have to take multi-vitamins or pharmaceuticals-promoted drugs to halt aging, hunger yourself, and thirst to reduce weight, or buy the latest products promising increased brain performance. According to several studies, adopting basic steps in the short term can result in longevity benefits.

# Chapter 4:

# *What if You Treated Your Life Like a Team Sport?*

Here's something we can all agree on: we want our lives to matter. We all want to live a satisfying, fulfilling, and purposeful life.

This isn't just a selfish desire. I believe that feeling a certain amount of significance in your life is healthy. It's good for the human experience. There is a healthy satisfaction that comes from contributing to the world around you. It's important to your physical and mental health.

But there is a problem.

Simply saying, "You need to live a life of purpose" doesn't help anyone. It's too abstract. Sure, I want to live a life of purpose, fulfillment, and significance ... but how do I translate that into action? I certainly don't have all the answers. (Big surprise.) But here's one thing that has helped me recently: I've been thinking about my own life as a team sport. Viewing my life in this context has helped me develop a clear plan and design real action steps for living a healthier, happier, and more fulfilling life.

Here's how I'm thinking about my life as a team sport and how you might find it useful as well.

**The Mission**

Every team has a mission that it strives to accomplish. A good team measures itself by something: wins, losses, championships. There is no Superbowl of Life, but I like thinking about my life in the same way.

How do you want your life to be *measured*? What do you want to be counted? What is a win? What is a loss? Additionally, just as a team needs the effort of every teammate to fulfill its mission, you need the help of those around you to fulfill your mission. How will the people on your "team" help you get to where you want to go? What role do your family, friends, and peers play in helping you achieve these goals? What about your teachers, your boss, and your mentors?

So often, we think about big questions like, "What do I want to do with my life?" without considering everyone else that we live with. Thinking about your life as a team sport forces you to realize an important lesson: your life is dramatically impacted by the people around you.

Life is a shared experience. And for this reason, the people around you need to be part of the plan. A good mission in life is always about more than just you.

**How I'm using this idea:** I often think about the mission of our team (and the mission of my life) when it comes to what we are building here. I'm working to change how we approach our health and use the science of behavior change and habit formation to make it easier for us to live healthy lives. And to do it, I need the support of my family and friends, the guidance of mentors and business partners, and the help of readers like you. It may have started as my idea, but it rapidly became our mission.

# Chapter 5:

# *How To Be Comfortable With*

# *Discomfort*

"The cure for pain is in the pain." - Rumi.

We've become so accustomed to living and striving for everyday life that if anything goes against it, our natural reaction is to ease it quickly. This doesn't only go for physical pain. We look for metaphorical medicine even when we feel emotional discomforts such as guilt, shame, or vulnerability. We dive into distractions instead of looking into the deeper causes of our emotional distresses. The avoidance of pain and discomfort has become a way of our lives.

We often mistake pleasure with happiness without knowing that satisfaction is brought to us by external factors while joy comes from within. It depends upon our views and perceptions of situations and people and something we always control. We have to make sure that we don't beat ourselves up with temporary distractions or reach for band-aids to avoid something uncomfortable. Turning distraction into opportunity and bringing yourself back to the present is what we should strive for. We should turn down our speed to a snail's pace because when we do something slower, it enables us to put in touch with our consciousness and physical sensations. It is then that we can dive into identifying the origin of our pain and where it resonates. We should be able to hang out with the hurt so we can begin to heal.

"What you resist, persists." - Carl Jung. The pain and discomfort that we feel act as messengers for us. If we avoid or cover them, they are bound to return. We should listen closely to what our pain is trying to tell us. Our happiness doesn't lie in eliminating painful situations; instead, it is connected to handling and perceiving them. We think that resistance is the only thing that will save us, but resistance is what makes us sink further into the hurt.

Pain hurts, and discomfort returns when we don't sit with them and get to know them. It's impressive to discover that many of our physical discomforts are brought on by our internal hurts like anxiety, stress, and loneliness. Once we recognize the true root of our pain, we can create a plan to heal the actual wound instead of placing metaphorical band-aids on it. It's better to breathe and connect your body to your mind to enforce control over your thoughts. This will help you handle any situation or crisis with betterment the next time it arises.

# Chapter 6:

# Enjoying The Journey

Today I want to talk about why enjoying the journey of life is important. And why hurrying to get to the destination might not be all that enjoyable as we think it is.

A lot of us plan our lives around an end goal, whether it be getting to a particular position in our company's ladder, or becoming the best player in a sport, or having the most followers on Instagram or whatever the goal may be... Many of us just can't wait to get there. However, many a times, once we reach our goal, whilst we may feel a sense of satisfaction and accomplishment for a brief moment, we inevitably feel like something is missing again and we search for our next objective and target to hit.

I have come to realise that in life, it is not always so much the end goal, but the journey, trials, struggles, and tribulations that make the journey there worth it. If we only focus on the end goal, we may miss out the amazing sights along the way. We will ultimately miss the point of the journey and why we embarked on it in the first place.

Athletes who achieve one major title never stop at just that one, they look for the next milestone they can achieve, but they enjoy the process, they take it one step at a time and at the end of their careers they can look back with joy that they had left no stone unturned. And that they can live their life without regret.

How many times have you seen celebrities winning the biggest prize in their careers, whether it may be the Grammy's Album of the Year if you are a musician, or the Oscars Best Actor or Best Actress Award. How many of them actually feel like that is the end of the journey? They keep creating and keep making movies and film not because they want that award, even though it is certainly a nice distinction to have, but more so because they enjoy their craft and they enjoy the art of producing.

If winning that trophy was the end goal, we would see many artists just end their careers there and then after reaching the summit. However that is not the case. They will try to create something new for as long as people are engaged with their craft, as with the case of Meryl Streep, even at 70+ she is still working her butt off even after she has achieve all the fame and money in the world.

Even for myself, at times i just want to reach the end as quickly as possible. But many times when i get there, i am never satisfied. I feel empty inside and i feel that I should be doing more. And when i rush to the end, i do feel like I missed many important sights along the way that would have made the journey much more rewarding and enjoyable had I told myself to slow it down just a little.

I believe that for all of us, the journey is much more important than the destination. It is through the journey that we grow as a person, it is through the journey that we evolve and take on new ideas, work ethics, knowledge, and many little nuggets that make the trip worth it at the end. If someone were to hand you a grand slam title without having you earned it, it would be an empty trophy with no meaning and emotions behind it. The trophy would not represent the hours of hard work that you have put in to be deserving of that title.

So I challenge each and everyone of you today to take a step back in whatever journey you may be on. To analyse in what aspects can you enjoy the moment and to not place so much pressure into getting to the destination asap. Take it one day at a time and see how the journey you are on is actually a meaningful one that you should treasure each day and not let up.

I hope you enjoyed today's topic and sharing and as always I wish you all the best in your endeavours. I'll see you in the next one.

# Chapter 7:

# *The Downside of Work-Life*

# *Balance*

One way to think about work-life balance is with a concept known as The Four Burners Theory. Here's how it was first explained to me:

Imagine that a stove represents your life with four burners on it. Each burner symbolizes one major quadrant of your life.

1. The first burner represents your family.

2. The second burner is your friends.

3. The third burner is your health.

4. The fourth burner is your work.

**The Four Burners Theory** says that "to be successful, you have to cut off one of your burners. And to be successful, you have to cut off two."
**The View of the Four Burners**

My initial reaction to The Four Burners Theory was to search for a way to bypass it. "Can I succeed and keep all four burners running?" I wondered.

Perhaps I could combine two burners. "What if I lumped family and friends into one category?"

Maybe I could combine health and work. "I hear sitting all day is unhealthy. What if I got a standing desk?" Now, I know what you are thinking. Believing that you will be healthy because you bought a standing desk is like believing you are a rebel because you ignored the fasten seatbelt sign on an airplane, but whatever.

Soon I realized I was inventing these workarounds because I didn't want to face the real issue: life is filled with tradeoffs. If you want to excel in your work and your marriage, then your friends and your health may have to suffer. If you want to be healthy and succeed as a parent, then you might be forced to dial back your career ambitions. Of course, you are free to divide your time equally among all four burners, but you have to accept that you will never reach your full potential in any given area.

Essentially, we are forced to choose. Would you rather live a life that is unbalanced but high-performing in a certain area? Or would you rather live a life that is balanced but never maximizes your potential in a given quadrant?

**Option 1: Outsource Burners**

We outsource small aspects of our lives all the time. We buy fast food, so we don't have to cook. We go to the dry cleaners to save time on laundry. We visit the car repair shop, so we don't have to fix our automobile.

Outsourcing small portions of your life allow you to save time and spend it elsewhere. Can you apply the same idea to one quadrant of your life and free up time to focus on the other three burners?

Work is the best example. For many people, work is the hottest burner on the stove. It is where they spend the most time, and it is the last burner to get turned off. In theory, entrepreneurs and business owners can outsource the work burner. They do it by hiring employees.

The Four Burners Theory reveals a truth everyone must deal with: nobody likes being told they can't have it all, but everyone has constraints on their time and energy. Every choice has a cost.

Which burners have you cut off?

# Chapter 8:

## *Six Habits of Self-Love*

We can show gratitude to ourselves for our different achievements in many ways. It is something that most people overlook as a waste of time and resources. This is a fallacy. It is high time we develop habits of self-love, to recharge our bodies and minds in preparation for another phase of achievements.

Here are six habits of self-love:

### 1. Treating Yourself

It is showing gratitude to yourself by way of satisfying your deepest desires instead of waiting for someone else to do it for you. Take the personal initiative to go shopping and buy that designer suit or dress you have been wanting so badly. Do not wait for someone else to do it for you while you are capable.

Take that much-needed vacation and a break from work to be with your family. Spend time with the people you love and cherish every moment because, in this fast-moving world, the future is uncertain. Secure your happiness lest you drown in depression. The best person to take care of your interests is yourself.

Who will take you out for swimming or outing to those posh hotels if you do not initiate it? Self-love begins when you realize your worth and do not allow anyone else to bring it down.

## 2. Celebrate Your Victories

Take advantage of every opportunity to celebrate your wins, no matter how small. A habit of self-love is to celebrate your achievements and ignore voices that discourage you. Nothing should muffle you from shouting your victories to the world. The testimony of your victory will encourage a stranger not to give up in his/her quest.

It is neither pride nor boastfulness. It is congratulating yourself for the wins that you rightfully deserve. How else can you love yourself if you do not appreciate yourself for the milestones you have conquered? Do not shy away from thanking yourself, privately or publicly, because no one else best knows your struggles except yourself.

## 3. Accept Yourself

To begin with, accept your social and economic status because you know the battles you have fought. Self-acceptance is an underrated form of self-love. Love yourself and accept your shortcomings. When you learn to accept yourself, other people will in turn accept you. They will learn how to accommodate you in the same manner you learned to live with all your imperfections.

Self-loathing dies when you master self-acceptance and self-love. Self-care keeps off self-rejection. You begin seeing your worth and great potential. It is the enemy within that is responsible for the fall of great empires.

The enemy within is low self-esteem and self-rejection. Accept the things you cannot change and change the things in your ability. Do not be hard on yourself because a journey of a thousand miles begins with a single step.

### 4. Practice Forgiveness

Forgiveness is a strong act. When you forgive those who wrong you, you let go of unnecessary baggage. It is unhealthy to live with a heart full of hate (pun intended). Forgiveness does not mean that you have allowed other people to wrong you repetitively. It means you have outgrown their wrong acts and you no longer allow their inconsiderate acts to affect you. Forgiveness benefits the forgiver more than the forgiven. It heals the heart from any hurt caused. It is the best form of self-care yet difficult at the same time. Forgiveness is a gradual process initiated by the bigger person in any conflict. Practicing self-care is by recognizing the importance of turning a new leaf and staying free from shackles of grudges and bitterness.

Unforgiveness builds bitterness and vengeance. It finally clouds your judgment and you become irrational. Choosing forgiveness is a vote on self-care.

### 5. Choose Your Associates Wisely

Associate with progressive people. Show me your friends and I will tell you the kind of person you are. Your friends have the potential to either build or destroy your appreciation of self-worth. They will trim your excesses and supplement your deficiencies. A cadre of professionals tends to share several traits.

Self-care involves taking care of your mental state and being selective of who you let into your personal space. It supersedes all other interests.

### 6. Engaging In Hobbies

Hobbies are the activities we do during our free time to relax our minds and bond with our friends. When doing these hobbies we are at ease and free from pressures of whatever form. We need to take a break from our daily work routine from time to time and do other social activities.

Hobbies are essential to explore other interests and rejuvenate our psyche and morale. Self-love places your interests and well-being above everything else. There is a thin line between it and selfishness, but it is not the latter.

These six habits of self-love will ensure you have peace and sobriety of mind to make progressive decisions.

# Chapter 9:

# 10 Habits of Kobe Bryant

Throughout 20 seasons, the late Kobe Bryant earned a reputation as the greatest basketball player of all time with the Los Angeles Lakers. The six-foot-six shooting guard dominated the court in NBA history, winning five NBA titles, a record of 18 consecutive All-Star Game selections, four All-Star Game MVP Awards, and the Academy Award for Best Animated Short Film, "Dear Basketball."

Bryant's off-court legacy was similarly outstanding, with record earnings for an NBA player, winning investments, and a lucrative shoe deal that increased his net worth to more than $600 million. He was also renowned for his strong work ethic. Highly applauded, you'll find endless stories on his 20-year career work ethics from his teammates, competitors, coaches, and other acquaintances.

Here are 10 Kobe Bryant's habits.

## 1. His Work Ethics

Kobe Bryant was well-known for having a solid work ethic. If he ever lost a game, he could figure out why and spend extra time improving. Losing a shot for Kobe meant training for hours and days until he couldn't miss it anymore. He was going to train so hard that you wouldn't beat him.

## 2. Become Obsessive

Kobe not only obsessed on basketball, but also dedicated his energy on becoming the best in every manner. "If you want to be exceptional at something, you have to obsess over it," he once said. That's precisely the mind set you need if you want to be the best in your field. Embrace your obsession, fall in love with the process, and use it to reach heights that others cannot.

## 3. Mamba Attitude

Kobe was determined to be one of the greatest basketballers at only 13 years of age. He said in an interview that he was inspired by great players like Michael Jordan and Magic Jordan. He would watch them play and wonder, "Can I get to that level?" "i don't know," he could say, "but let's find out." Whether you're starting a business, becoming a great athlete, learning a new skill, or forming a new habit, modelling your habits after someone who has already succeeded will save you the most time and money in the long run.

## 4. Compete Against Yourself

When you compete with yourself, you put others in the position to keep up with you. Kobe never had this problem because he fought within him to be the type of athlete who could win more after winning his first championship. Throughout his career, he progressed from being the No. 8 Kobe who wanted to win to the No. 24 Kobe who needed to be a leader and a better teammate.

## 5. Embracing New Abilities

After Kobe retired from sports in 2016, his next focus was on finding ways to inspire the world through diverse stories, characters, and leadership. He pushed and founded multimedia production company Granity Studios, which is 2018, lead to his Academy Award- a Sports Emmy and an Annie Award for his short animated film Dear Basketball. Embracing new skills will keep your legacy going and diversify your abilities in different walks of life.

## 6. Leaders develop leaders

"I enjoyed testing people and making them uncomfortable," Kobe once said. "That is what leads to introspection, which leads to improvement. I guess you could say I challenged them to be their best selves." On the court, Kobe was a strong, albeit contentious, leader for his team.

## 7. Handling the Pressure is Everything

When you're under pressure, you're forced to make critical choices and decisions. Sometimes, you'll make the wrong decisions, but that what keeps you going strong. When Kobe was playing against the Utah Jazz at 18 years, he missed a shot which led to his team losing the game. This had him working on the shot during the entire off-season.

## 8. Perseverance

Kobe's success was as a result of sticking to his process through perseverance. He was determined not to give in to anyone or anything that pushed him backwards. Your strength to keep moving will eventually payoff.

## 9. Failure Begets Growth

Failure is only ideal when you keep learning. In an interview, Kobe mentioned being an 11-year-old basketball player who played in a summer league for an entire season without scoring a single point! Really?! So he had to work extra for the following ten months to become a better shot and learn how to score.

## 10.Passion Is Everything

It's undeniable that Kobe had a strong love and enthusiasm for basketball. His passion for basketball, his work ethic, and competitiveness helped him become a five-time champion. When you sincerely love your craft, and put more into it, you will always rise against the odds to achieve success.

## Conclusion

Although Bryant was an exceptional talent, his success was a product of an intense, obsessive work ethic. Bryant's desire to be the best was evident in almost every aspect of his life.

# Chapter 10:

# *How to Value Being Alone*

Some people are naturally happy alone. But for others, being solo is a challenge. If you fall into the latter group, there are ways to become more comfortable with being alone (yes, even if you're a hardcore extrovert).

Regardless of how you feel about being alone, building a good relationship with yourself is a worthy investment. After all, you *do* spend quite a bit of time with yourself, so you might as well learn to enjoy it.

**Being alone isn't the same as being lonely.**

Before getting into the different ways to find happiness in being alone, it's important to untangle these two concepts: being alone and being lonely. While there's some overlap between them, they're completely different concepts. Maybe you're a person who basks in solitude. You're not antisocial, friendless, or loveless. You're just quite content with alone time. You look forward to it. That's simply being alone, not being lonely.

On the other hand, maybe you're surrounded by family and friends but not relating beyond a surface level, which has you feeling empty and disconnected. Or maybe being alone just leaves you sad and longing for company. That's loneliness.

**Short-term tips to get you started**

These tips are aimed at helping you get the ball rolling. They might not transform your life overnight, but they can help you get more comfortable with being alone.

Some of them may be exactly what you needed to hear. Others may not make sense to you. Use them as stepping-stones. Add to them and shape them along the way to suit your lifestyle and personality.

## 1. Avoid comparing yourself to others.

This is easier said than done, but try to avoid comparing your social life to anyone else's. It's not the number of friends you have or the frequency of your social outings that matters. It's what works for you.

Remember, you have no way of knowing if someone with many friends and a stuffed social calendar is happy.

## 2. Take a step back from social media.

Social media isn't inherently bad or problematic, but if scrolling through your feeds makes you feel left out and stresses, take a few steps back. That feed doesn't tell the whole story. Not by a long shot.

You have no idea if those people are truly happy or just giving the impression that they are. Either way, it's no reflection on you. So, take a <u>deep breath</u> and put it in perspective.

Perform a test run and ban yourself from social media for 48 hours. If that makes a difference, try giving yourself a daily limit of 10 to 15 minutes and stick to it.

**Don't be afraid to ask for help.**

Sometimes, all the self-care, exercise, and gratitude lists in the world aren't enough to shake feelings of sadness or loneliness.

Consider reaching out to a therapist if:

- You're overly <u>stressed</u> and finding it difficult to cope.

- You have <u>symptoms of anxiety</u>.

- You have <u>symptoms of depression</u>.

You don't have to wait for a crisis point to get into <u>therapy</u>. Simply wanting to get better and spending time alone is a perfectly good reason to make an appointment.

# PART 2

# Chapter 1:

# How to Love Yourself First

It's so easy to tell someone "Love yourself" and much more difficult to describe *how* to do it. Learn and practice these six steps to gradually start loving yourself more every day:

**Step 1: Be willing to feel pain and take responsibility for your feelings.**

Step 1 is mindfully following your breath to become present in your body and embrace all of your feelings. It's about moving toward your feelings rather than running away from them with various forms of self-abandonment, such as staying focused in your head, judging yourself, turning to addictions to numb out, etc. All feelings are informational.

**Step 2: Move into the intent to learn.**

Commit to learning about your emotions, even the ones that may be causing you pain, so that you can move into taking loving action.

**Step 3: Learn about your false beliefs.**

Step 3 is a deep and compassionate process of exploration—learning about your beliefs and behavior and what is happening with a person or situation that may be causing your pain. Ask your feeling self, your inner child: "What am I thinking or doing that's causing the painful feelings of anxiety, depression, guilt, shame, jealousy, anger, loneliness, or emptiness?" Allow the answer to come from inside, from your intuition and feelings.

Once you understand what you're thinking or doing that's causing these feelings, ask your ego about the fears and false beliefs leading to the self-abandoning thoughts and actions.

## Step 4: Start a dialogue with your higher self.

It's not as hard to connect with your higher guidance as you may think. The key is to be open to learning about loving yourself. The answers may come immediately or over time. They may come in words or images or dreams. When your heart is open to learning, the answers will come.

## Step 5: Take loving action.

Sometimes people think of "loving myself" as a feeling to be conjured up. A good way to look at loving yourself is by emphasizing the action: "What can I *do* to love myself?" rather than "How can I *feel* love for myself?"

By this point, you've already opened up to your pain, moved into learning, started a dialogue with your feelings, and tapped into your spiritual guidance. Step 5 involves taking one of the loving actions you identified in Step 4. However small they may seem at first, over time, these actions add up.

**Step 6: Evaluate your action and begin again as needed.**

Once you take the loving action, check in to see if your pain, anger, and shame are getting healed. If not, you go back through the steps until you discover the truth and loving actions that bring you peace, joy, and a deep sense of intrinsic worth.

Over time, you will discover that loving yourself improves everything in your life—your relationships, health and well-being, ability to manifest your dreams, and self-esteem. Loving and connecting with yourself is the key to loving and connecting with others and creating loving relationships. Loving yourself is the key to creating a passionate, fulfilled, and joyful life.

# Chapter 2:

## *How To Have Proper Time Management*

Managing time is one of the hardest things to do; our everyday routine revolves around time management. But what does it mean? Some people fail to understand the true meaning of time management. Time management can be defined as planning and controlling how much time to spend on specific activities. When a person knows how to manage his time, he faces less stress and efficiently completes more work in less time.

Everyone now wants to manage their time, the world is moving fast, so must we, but how to do that? The answer is relatively easy. You need to set your goals correctly. Setting your goals correctly would help you save time and so your brain wouldn't be messed up. The SMART method is the best method, where s stands for specific, M stands for measurable, A stands for attainable, R stands for relevant, and T stands for timely. If you set your goals by using the SMART method, you are bound to manage your time.

Now sometimes we all have so much work to do that we forget which one is more important, what you should do is to sit back for a minute, take out your to-do list and see which of your daily task is both important as well as urgent than that task should be your priority and you should do these tasks right away. Some tasks are important but not urgent, you can decide when to do these, but some are neither critical nor urgent you can leave them later to do. Prioritizing your tasks properly helps you manage time.

We all say that this generation is moving fast, but we also know that laziness is in the air. Being lazy is what messes up our routine. "Time is money" we all have heard this but hardly pay attention to this; wasting our time on one task is like ruining our whole plan for the day. You need to set a time limit for every task, depending on its difficulty level. When you have been assigned something to do, estimate the time it would take you to complete that task and set a limit. If you think you don't have enough time to complete the task, then seeking help from someone is not a bad option. But if you don't check the time, you may end up with incomplete work that will cause you a few problems.

Although work is essential, "All work and no play makes Jack a dull boy," this means that when a person is constantly working and burdens himself with the workload, he finds it hard to concentrate because his brain is all fried up. When you have a busy and packed schedule that includes many tasks, try to take small breaks between these tasks. Working constantly will make it hard for you to focus on your next task. You should take a break in the middle of these tasks, try grabbing a brief nap, or you can do something that will freshen up your brain like meditation, jogging, etc.

An organized person feels less messed up; for example, even if your wardrobe is messed up, you feel uncomfortable because this nagging sensation at the back of your head tells you that your closet needs to be organized. Similarly, try managing your calendar for more long-term time management. Try writing on a calendar about appointments, meetings, deadlines, so you don't forget what to do next. If there is something you need to do, then set a few days for that specific task. This method will help you remember more of your task and your plans.

Although time management is hard, it is not impossible. You just need to prioritise, take small breaks and sort out everything and you would be good to go.

# Chapter 3:

# Happy People Celebrate Other People's Success

What a phony smile… Why do people want him? How has he accomplished anything? It's ME they need. I'm the one who should be successful, not him. What a joke." This was my inner dialogue when I heard about other people's success. Like a prima donna, I seethed with jealousy and couldn't stand to hear about people doing better than me.

But all the hating got me nowhere. So I thought about who I was really mad at…it wasn't the successful people I raged at. When I got more serious about succeeding, I channeled that useless envy into accepting myself.

I practiced self-acceptance with a journal, through affirmations, and by encouraging myself—especially when I failed. Then something weird happened. I started feeling happy for other people's success. Without a hint of irony, I congratulated people on their hard work, and I applauded their success with my best wishes. It felt good. I felt more successful doing it.

> **"Embrace your uniqueness. Time is much too short to be living someone else's life." – Kobi Yamada**

My writing career caught fire at the same time. I was published on sites that I'd only dreamt of, and whose authors I had cussed for doing things that the egotistical me still hadn't. Congratulating others started a positive feedback loop. The more I accepted myself, the more I celebrated other people's success and the more I celebrated their success, the more success I achieved. Now that I look back, I could've hacked my growth curve by celebrating others' success as a daily ritual.

### 1.  It conditions you for your own success

Feeling good for someone else's success helps you generate the same feelings you need for your own accomplishments. So put yourself in the other's shoes. Revel in their accomplishments; think of all the hard work that went into it. Celebrate their success and know that soon you'll experience the same thing for yourself. Apply the good feelings to your visions for a brighter future.

### 2.  You'll transcend yourself

Everyone knows that to actually succeed, you need to be part of something bigger. But most people are kept from that bigger something by wanting all the focus for themselves. it's an ego issue.

Through celebrating others, you'll practice the selflessness it takes to let go of your tiny shell and leap into the ocean of success that comes through serving others. Cheer your fellow entrepreneurs. Feel their success. Let go of your want for recognition and accept that you'll get it when you help enough other people.

# Chapter 4:

# Discovering Your Purpose

If you guys don't already know, this is one of the topics that I really love talking about. And I never get tired of it. Having a purpose is something that I always believe everyone should have. Having a purpose to live, to breathe, to get up each day, I believe that without purpose, there is no point to life.

So today we're going to talk about how to discover your purpose, and why you should make it a point to find one if you didn't already start looking.

So what is purpose exactly. A purpose is a reason to do something. Is to have something else greater than ourselves to work for. You see, I believe if we are only focused on ourselves, instead of others, we will not be able to be truly happy in life. Feeding our own self interests does not bring us joy as one might think. After living the life that I had, I realized that true happiness only comes when you bring joy to someone else's life. Whether it be helping others professionally or out of selflessness, this happiness will radiate and reflect back to us from someone else who is appreciative of your efforts.

On some level, we can look into ourselves to be happy. For example being grateful for life, loving ourselves, and all that good stuff. Yes keep doing those things. But there is a whole other dimension if we devote our time and energy into helping others once we have already conquered ourselves. If you look at many of the most successful people on the planet, after they have acquired an immense amount of wealth, many of them look to passion projects or even philanthropy where they can give back to the community when having more money doesn't do anything for them anymore. If you look at Elon Musk and Jeff Bezos, these two have a greater purpose which is their space projects. Where they visualise humans being able to move out of Earth one day where civilisation is able to expand. Or Bill Gates and Warren Buffet, who have pledged to give billions of their money away for philanthropic work, to help the less fortunate and to fund organisations that work towards finding cures to diseases.

Now for us mere mortals, we don't need to think so big. Our purpose need not be so extravagant. It can be as simple as having a purpose to provide for your loved one, to work hard to bring your family members of holidays and travel, or to bring joy to your elderly relatives by organising activities for them to do. There is no purpose that is too big or too small.

Your purpose could be helping others find a beautiful home, doing charitable work, or even feeding and providing for your growing family.

As humans, we will automatically work harder if we have a clear and defined purpose. We have a reason to get up each day, to go to work, to earn that paycheck, so that we can spend it on things and people, even ourselves at times. Without a purpose, we struggle to find meaning in the work that we do. We struggle to see the big picture and we find that we have no reason to work so hard, or even at all. And we struggle to find life worth living.

This revelation came to me when I started seeing my work as helping some other person in a meaningful way. Where my work was not just about making money to buy nice things, but to be able to impact someone else's life in a positive way. That became my purpose. To see them learn something new, and to bring a joy and smile to their faces. That thought that I was contributing something useful to someone made me smile more than money ever could. Yes money can help you live a comfortable life, but helping others can go a much farther way into giving your life true purpose.

So I challenge each and everyone of you to find a purpose in everything that you do, and if you struggle to find one, start by making the goal to help others a priority. Think of the difference you can make to others and that could very well be your purpose in life as well.

I believe in each and every one of you.. I hope you learned something today and as always, take care and I'll see you in the next one.

# Chapter 5:

## 10 Habits of Rafael Nadal

Rafael Nadal is a Spanish professional tennis player famously known as "The King of Clay" because of his dominance and success on the tennis court. He is currently ranked No. 4 in the world by the ATP, with previous records as No. 1 in the ATP rankings for 209 weeks, and has closed the year as No. 1 five times.

Great champions are born with the ability to persevere in the face of adversity, including fear, suffering, self-doubt, and helplessness. Rafael Nadal proved this yet again by fighting like a gladiator to win his 13th French Open title and 20th Major overall at the just-concluded Roland Garros event. You don't achieve that kind of reputation unless you're continuously humble, hardworking, and producing exceptional outcomes.

Here are ten habits of Rafael Nadal.

### 1. Neurotic on-Court Habits

Before every match, Nadal has made it a habit of taking cold showers, towels down after even aces, and double points. He points the labels of his drinking bottles at the end of the court he's about to play from and never stands up from his chair before his opponent. If you're not this neurotic, you'll never made it to the Wimbledon Final.

## 2. Trophies Are a Product of Well-Earned Practice

Despite your incredible athlete talents and abilities, as Rafael notes, is not enough to secure a win over 13 French Opens. But careful and intensive practice does. His workout routine is based on Anders Ericsson's "10,000-hour rule" for court success.

## 3. Focus

Alongside hard work, you need focus. Rafa plays every point as if his life depends on it. Extraordinary outcomes depend on your concentration on winning points.

## 4. Every Strike Counts

Rafael is constantly putting himself in the best winning position for each point, game, and set. Rafael on his serve says: "It's not just about your serving ideas but also your positioning, speed variation, and spin." It definitely gets better!

## 5. Be Self-Assured

Nadal is not of those athletes who focus on self-doubt thoughts even while going against a competitive rival on the court. Self-confidence is the most crucial variable in sports and performance psychology.

## 6. Excellence Is a Habit

Work hard every day; as Rafa puts it, when you wake up motivated to intense workout and practice, you'll always excel in your performance tactics. Rafa understands that the most challenging work begins right before his next match, and he has one goal, "enjoy your game while playing, and always strive on improving."

## 7. You Can't Succeed on Your Own

No matter your dedicated you are, you never win anything on your own. For the same reason, Nadal always has his Uncle Toni, his family, and friends by his side. Uncle Toni has taught him how to be mentally tough to succeed. To become an elite athlete, you'll have to learn and practice patience, put up with whatever comes your way, overcome weakness and agony, and push yourself to the limit.

## 8. Serve Others

In 2008 he launched the Rafa Nadal Foundation, known for its social and personal aid for less in Spain and India. He believes sport opens the doors to a better future. Becoming a star is one thing, but portraying your humanity trait makes it better.

## 9. Grit

Angela Lee defines grit as "passion and tenacity for very long-term goals." Grit is endurance and commitment to your future. As a tennis player, you can win and lose, and you must be prepared for both. However, as you get older, both winning and losing become easier. That is what characterizes Nadal's tennis. In every match, whether he wins or loses, his will and determination to battle till the end distinguish him.

## 10. Tournaments End. Dedication, Does Not

When you're down two sets, remember to keep calm, even when people cheering you up are freaking out and worried about you. According to Rafa, "the only way to achieve this is to fight back, move, run, and control that pressure." Every time Rafa enters the court, he leaves with a new found hunger and gives his all in every point, regardless of whether he is playing against a qualifier or the greatest of all.

## Conclusion

Rafa plays hard wherever and whenever he plays. He is adamant. He is tenacious and plays for the love of the game. You may argue that all records are supposed to be broken, and all athletic events are just games. Still, they're also about leaving a legacy, accepting and expressing pride in one's abilities.

# Chapter 6:

# Happy People Are Optimistic

Beyond the simple reality that optimists are happier people (and happiness is what you're striving for), optimism has other benefits as well. So, if you want to achieve greater happiness, try being optimistic for a day.

**Optimists enjoy a greater degree of academic success than pessimists do.** Because optimistic students think it's possible for them to make a good grade, they study hardier and they study smarter. They manage the setting in which they study and they seek help from others when they need it. (Optimism, it turns out, is almost as predictive of how well students do in college as the SAT.)

**Optimists are more self-confident than pessimists are.** They believe in *themselves* more than fate.

**Optimists are more likely to be problem-solvers than pessimists are.** When pessimistic students get a D on a test, they tend to think things like: "I knew I shouldn't have taken this course. I'm no good at psychology." The optimistic student who gets a D says to herself, "I can do better. I just didn't study enough for this test. I'll do better next time." And she will.

**Optimists welcome second chances after they fail more than pessimists do.** Optimistic golfers always take a *mulligan* (a redo swing without penalty). Why? Because they expect to achieve a better result the second time around.

**Optimists are more socially outgoing than pessimists are.** Socially outgoing folks believe that the time they spend with other human beings makes them better in some way — smarter, more interesting, more attractive. Unfortunately, pessimists see little, if any, benefit from venturing out into the social world.

**Optimists are not as lonely as pessimists are.** Because pessimists don't see as much benefit from socializing with others, they have far fewer social and emotional connections in their lives, which is what loneliness is all about.

**Optimists utilize social support more effectively than pessimists do.** They aren't afraid to reach out in times of need.

**Optimists are less likely to blame others for their misfortune than pessimists are.** When you blame someone else for your troubles, what you're really saying is, "You're the *cause* of my problem and, therefore, you have to be the *solution* as well." Optimists have just as many troubles as pessimists throughout life — they just accept more responsibility for dealing with their misfortune.

**Optimists cope with stress better than pessimists do.** Pessimists worry, optimists act. A patient with coronary heart disease who is pessimistic "hopes and prays" that he doesn't have another heart attack anytime soon. The optimistic heart patient leaves little to chance — instead, he exercises regularly, practices his meditation exercises, adheres to a low-cholesterol diet, and makes sure he always gets a good night's sleep.

# Chapter 7:

## 10 Habits That Can Ruin Your Day

Habits are the building blocks of our day. No matter how you spin it, either way, every detail matters.

The little actionable habits eventually sets you up to a either having a fulfilling day, or one that you have just totally wasted away. Nothing is as bad as destructive habits as they sabotage your daily productivity. Slowly, you slip further and further until it's too late when you've realized the damage that they have done to your life.

Bad habits are insidious! They drag down your life, lowers down your levels of accuracy, and make your performance less creative and stifling.

It is essential, not only for productivity, to gain control of your bad habits. AS Grenville Kleiser once noted, "Constant self-discipline and self-control help you develop greatness of character." Nonetheless, it is important to stop and ask: what do you need today to get rid of or change? Sure, you can add or adjust new skills into your daily life.

Below are ten persistent habits that can ruin your day's success and productivity.

## 1. Hitting The Snooze Button.

Your mind, while you sleep, moves through a comprehensive series of cycles, the last one alerting you to wake up. While you crave for ten more minutes of sleep as the alarm goes off, what do you do? You whacked the snooze button. We're all guilty of this! If you don't suck it up, rip off the cover and start your morning, the rest of your day will be flawed. How do you expect your day to be strong once you don't start it off strong? You will feel far more optimistic, strong and fully prepared when you wake up without hitting the snooze button. So avoid the snooze button at any cost if you want a productive day ahead!

## 2. Wasting Your "Getting Ready" Hours.

You might need to reconsider the scrolling of Instagram and Facebook or the inane program you put on behind the scenes while preparing. These things have a time and place to partake in them – for example when you've accomplished your day's work and need some time to unwind and relax; however the time isn't now. Your morning schedule ought to be an interaction that prepares and energizes you for the day ahead. The objective is to accomplish something that animates your mind within the first hour of being conscious, so you can be more inventive, invigorated, gainful, and connected with all through the entire day! Avoiding this sweeps you away from normalizing the worst habit you might have: distraction. Instead, give yourself a chance to breathe the fine morning, anticipate the day's wonder and be thankful for whatever you have.

## 3. Failing To Prioritize Your Breakfast.

Energizing your day is essential if you wish for a very productive day. Energizing your body system requires that you prioritize eating your breakfast. However, the contents of your breakfast must entail something that will ensure that your day is not slowed down by noon. This means a blend of high - fiber foods such as proteins and healthy must be incorporated. Avoid taking too many sugars and heavy starches. The goal is to satiate and energize your body for the day.

## 4. Ruminating on the Problems of Yesterday And Negativity.

Don't take yesterday's problems to your new day if you want to start your day off right. If the day before you had difficult meetings and talks and you woke up ruminating about your horrific experiences, leave that negativity at your doorway. Moreover, if the problem you are lamenting about have been solved, then you shouldn't dwell on the past. Research suggests that we usually encounter more positive than negative events in a day. Still, often your mind concentrates on the negative due to a subconscious distortion called the negative distortion. By choosing not to focus on negative events and thinking about what's going well, you can learn to take advantage of the strength of the positive events around us. Raising negativity only increases stress. Let go of it and get on without it!

## 5. Leaving Your Day To Randomness.

Do not let stuff just simply happen to you; do it. Failure to create a structured day leads to a totally random day. A random day lacking direction, focus, and efficiency. Distractions will also creep into your day more readily because you have allowed randomness to happen to you. Instead, have a clear and precise list of what you need to focus for the day. This serves as a framework and a boundary for you to work within. Another thing you should consider is to spend your first 90 minutes on the most thoughtful and important task for the day. This allows you to know the big things out right at the beginning, reducing your cognitive burden for the rest of the day.

## 6. Becoming Involved With the Overview.

How frequently have you woken up, and before you can stretch and grin, you groan pretty much all the have-to for now and the fragmented musts from yesterday? This unhealthy habit will ruin your great day ahead. Know and understand these are simply contemplations. You can decide to recalibrate by pondering all you must be thankful for and searching for the splendid focuses in your day. Shift thinking, and you'll begin the day empowered.

## 7. Overscheduling and Over-Engagement.

People tend to underestimate how long things take with so many things to do. This habit of overscheduling and over-engagement can quickly lead to burn out. Always ensure that you permit extra time and energy for the unforeseen. Take regular breaks and don't overcommit to other people. This gives you more freedom for yourself and you won't be running the risk of letting others down by not turning up. Try not to overestimate what you can complete, so you won't feel like a disappointment. Be sensible and practical with your scheduling. Unexpectedly and eventually, you'll complete more.

## 8. Postponing or Discarding the Tough Tasks.

We have a restricted measure of mental energy, and as we exhaust this energy, our dynamic and efficiency decrease quickly. This is called decision exhaustion. Running the bad habit of postponing and disregarding the tough tasks will trigger this reaction in us. At the point when you put off extreme assignments till late in the day because they're scary, you deplete more and more of your mental resources. To beat choice weariness, you should handle complex assignments toward the beginning of the day when your brain is new.

## 9. Failure To Prioritize Your Self-Care.

Work, family commitments, and generally talking of the general obligations give almost everyone an awesome excuse to let your self-care rehearses pass by the wayside. Achievement-oriented minds of individuals see how basic self-care is to their expert achievement. Invest energy doing things that bring you delight and backing your psychological and actual wellbeing. "Success" doesn't exclusively apply to your finances or expert accomplishments.

# 10. Waiting for the Easier Way Out / Waiting for the Perfect Hack of Your Life.

The most noticeably awful everyday habit is trusting that things will occur and for a chance to thump at your entryway. As such, you become an inactive onlooker, not a proactive part of your own life. Once in a while, it shows itself as the quest for simple little-known techniques. Rather than getting down to work, ineffective individuals search how to take care of job quicker for quite a long time. Try not to begin with a #lifehack search on the internet unless it really does improve your productivity without sacrificing the necessary steps you need to take each day to achieve holistic success.

## ✓ Merging It All Together

A portion of these habits may appear to be minor, yet they add up. Most amount to an individual decision between immediate pleasures and enduring ones. The most exceedingly awful propensity is forgetting about what matters to you. Always remember that you are just one habit away from changing you life forever.

# Chapter 8:

# Dealing With Addiction To

# Technology

Today we're going to talk about addiction to technology and media consumption. I think this is a topic that many of us can relate, even myself included. Am my goal for today is to try to help put forth a more sustainable and healthy habit for you to still enjoy technology while not being overwhelmed and overtaken by it completely.

So lets ask ourselves a simple question of why are we so hooked into using our devices so frequently and sparingly? I think for most of us, and this is my personal opinion, is that it offers us an escape, a distraction from our every day tasks that we know we ought to do. To procrastinate just a little bit or to binge scroll on Instagram, Facebook, Snapchat, and what have you, to satisfy our need for media consumption.

We use technology as a tool a gateway into the world of digital media, and we get lost in it because companies try to feed us with posts and stuff that we like to keep us engaged and to keep us watching just a little while longer. And minutes can turn into hours, and before you know it, it is bedtime.

I want to argue that this addiction is not entirely your fault, but that these multi billion dollar mega companies are being fed so much data that they are able to manipulate us into consume their media. It is like how casinos use various tricks of flickering lights, and free drinks to keep you playing a little longer and to spend a little more of your attention and time. We unknowingly get subjected to these manipulative tactics and we fall for it despite our best efforts to abstain from it.

I for one have been the subject of such manipulation. Whether it be Netflix or my favourite social media apps, I find myself mindlessly scrolling through posts trying to get my quick fix of distraction and supposed stress relief. However these feelings dont bring me joy, rather it brings me anxiety that I have wasted precious time and I end up kicking myself for it afterwards. This happens time and time again and it felt like I was stuck in a loop, unable to get out.

So what is the solution to this seemingly endless spiral of bad habits? Some might say just to delete the apps, or turn off wifi. But how many of you might have actually tried that yourself only to have it backfire on you? Redownloading the app is only one step away, wifi is only one button away, and addictions aren't so easily kicked to the curb as one might think.

What I have found that works is that instead of consuming mindless media that don't bring about actual benefit to my life, I chose to watch content that I could actually learn something from. Like this channel for example. I went on the hunt to seek out content that I could learn how to make extra money, how to improve my health, how to improve my relationships, basically anything that had to do with personal development. And I found that I actually felt less guilty watching or reading these posts even though they still do take up my time to consume.

You may call it a lesser of two evils, but what I discovered was that it provided much more benefit to my life than actually not consuming any personal development media at all. Whether it be inspirational stories from successful entrepreneurs like Elon Musk, or Jeff Bezos, or multi billion dollar investment advice from Warren Buffet, these passive watching of useful content actually boosted my knowledge in areas that I might otherwise have not been exposed to. Subconsciously, i started internalizing some of these beliefs and adopted it into my own psyche. And i transformed what was mindless binge watching of useless Tv shows and zombie content, to something that actually moved the needle in my life in the right direction, even by a little.

Overtime, I actually required less and less distraction of media consumption using my technology devices like iPhones and iPads or Macs, and started putting more attention and effort to do the work that I knew i had to get done. Because some of these personal development videos actually taught me what I needed to do to get stuff done and to stop procrastinating in working towards my goals.

So I challenge each and everyone of you today to do a thorough review of the kinds of music and media consumption that you consume today with your smartphones and tablets, and see if you can substitute them with something that you can learn from, no matter how trivial you think it may be. It could be the very push you need to start porting over all your bad habits of technology into something that can pay off for you 10 years down the road.

I hope you learned something today, and I'll see you in the next one.

# Chapter 9:

# 10 Habits of Michael Phelps

With 28 medals, 23 of which are gold, Michael Phelps is the greatest and most decorated Olympian in history. His career included five Olympic Games and two decades of supremacy. Even though Phelps competes in a sport where exceptionally talented athletes can win gold medals over various distances and strokes, his achievements dwarf those of any other athletes.

His competitive nature and a strong desire to always win have everything to do with his breakthrough. How did Phelps become the world's most excellent swimmer?

Here are the ten habits of Michael Phelps.

### 1. Dream Big and Set Outlandish Goals

According to Phelps, "the more you dream, and your goals, the more you achieve greatness." He desired a swimming career and had goals of becoming the best. He had to put in a lot of effort to attain his ambitions, including earning a gold medal at the Olympic Games. You won't achieve anything unless you dream big and set lofty aspirations.

### 2. Dare Doing New Things

Nothing is impossible, according to Phelps, as long as you are willing to try it out. Phelps understands how tough it is to win an Olympic gold medal, but he was motivated to do it and make history. Don't step back from trying new things because you are not sure of the outcomes.

### 3. Believe That Anything Is Possible

Phelps was able to become the finest swimmer in the world because he believed in himself. He also believes that God answers prayers of those who have faith and strive hard to achieve their goals. You must believe that anything is possible as you strive to achieve it.

### 4. Utilize Both Your Strengths and Weaknesses

Michael Phelps is well-known for his athleticism. His workouts are tough, and has best genetic attributes. However, he has ADHD and uses it as fuel for his swimming. Just like Phelps, your strengths and weaknesses are your biggest motivation.

### 5. Maintain Strict Self-Control

There is no quick way to greatness. You must put in the effort if you want to be successful at anything. For Phelps to be a world-class athlete, you must sustain world-class actions. He trains for 6 hours a day, seven days a week. When he is not doing physical training, he rests, allowing his muscles to relax while meditating and visualizing.

### 6. Don't Give Up

Michael Phelps is a real example of how you shouldn't allow your failures define or ruin you. Just triumph over them no matter what. Remember how Phelps' reputation was tarnished after he was detained from his drunk and drinking habits? Despite the anguish, he always came back strong.

## 7.  Get a Puppy

Phelps has a dog named Herman, a bulldog he adores and makes him more responsible. Moreover, it helps him in managing his ADHD. Having a pet makes you more accountable, empathic, compassionate, and disciplined.

## 8.  Give It Your Best

Phelps physical traits-his hands and feet can function as paddles, and his height form glides effortlessly through the water. For sure, he was a swimmer! Michael learned of his exceptional talent and persisted in becoming an Olympic champion. It would be great if you always practiced what you are best at to excel in it.

## 9.  Survive the Odds for Success

When his career was setting off, Phelps achieved zero notable positions. He lost in several championships, which crushed him as a young swimmer. He did not, however, quit. He trained harder than ever before, and in the 2008 Beijing Olympics, he won eight gold medals, breaking the record for the most gold medals won in a single sport. Hung in there, despite the setbacks, persevere, and eventually, you'll triumph.

## 10. Be Self-Assured Enough To Declare Your Aspirations

There was no doubt that Michael was born to be a legend, and he was not afraid to let the world know about it. His pride in letting people know his plans to win several gold medals was constantly chastised as arrogance, but his fans always had his back. Yes, there will be sceptics, but letting your friends and family in to a portion of your goals keep you motivated.

## Conclusion

There is doubt that Michael Phelps is an excellent swimmer and a champion given that he has set and broken several world records. Just like Phelps, your career, personal life, and other areas of your life will be defined by your daily routine. His habits are definitely a 100% worth of mentoring you towards being the best you can be.

# Chapter 10:

## 10 Habits of Lewis Hamilton

One thing is certain about Lewis Hamilton: he is a legend. He is a four-time Formula One World Champion who knows how to win on the track and in life. He is widely lauded as one of the best drivers of his generation, if not all time. In 2008, he became the youngest champion in history, winning the final turn of the season's final race.

He raced in Formula One for three decades, winning a record-equalling seven world championships, triple-figure pole positions, and a knighthood. You're surely aware that Lewis oozes driving talent, but there's much more to Hamilton than what he does behind the wheel.

Here are the ten habits of Lewis Hamilton.

### 1. Executes Under Pressure

Racing drivers like Lewis must control and remain calm despite driving at speeds up to 230 miles per hour in a sports car that may reach temperatures of 50 degrees. With limited space and vision, you can imagine how hectic it is for him to composure himself to adapt, make split-second decisions, and win.

### 2. Keep Your Eyes on the Price

As a child, Lewis always wanted to be a race car driver. He even met his future boss, Ron Dennis, as a toddler and promised him that he'd be racing his cars in the future. With his attention and persistence, he was able to turn that goal into reality. How determined and focused are you in attaining your goals? Keep your eventual aim in sight at all times!

## 3. Technology Is Everything

Formula one racing is a technology-driven sport in which a minor flaw in the car can alter the race's outcome. Hamilton and his team are always ahead of others with well-researched data for optimizing his performance. To place your content in the driver's seat for success, it must be easily available, properly categorized, and in the proper format, which is why the platform you deal with must be intelligent, smart, and dependable.

## 4. Discipline Pays Off

Lewis Hamilton is one of the world's most disciplined athletes. While some people may not consider Formula one racing to be a sport in which you must be in peak physical condition to be successful, Lewis treats his physical fitness as a shrine for his mental health lucidity as mental health is key to racing. His commitment to healthy food and consistent training has helped him win 43 Formula One races throughout his career.

## 5. Put in the Effort

Lewis is all about dedication to excellence. "You start training in December, start testing at the end of January and through the entire month of February, and then you go to the season," he explained. You're always on the move. How committed are you to attain your most important goals? Small steps lead to big steps, and big steps lead to bigger steps.

## 6. Dispatch, Adapt and Enhance

When Lewis achieves something, he celebrates his victory debriefing, analyses his performance, and learns how they may have improved their racing plan. Lewis Hamilton is the best because of his relentless, determined pursuit of perfection. It would be best to always debrief with a reliable team, react to problems and develop your techniques, and stay ahead of the competition.

## 7. Physical and Mental Health First

Lewis is always trying to stay optimistic and healthy for his body, mind, soul, and spirit. It's hard to step back from doing something you love most but look at the bigger picture. Instead of grumbling or worrying about the future, step back and examine yourself-accessing and confronting your current issues.

## 8. Keep the Right People

While it appears that you get to tour the world and explore in Formula One, you spend more time alone. Lewis spends most of his time with

Angela-his best friend, trainer, and physiotherapist. She exudes positive energy and always keeps him strong and motivated, so he can focus on remaining competitive.

## 9.  Don't Gauge Yourself Against Others.

Lewis doesn't consider other drivers in terms of inspiration, motivation, or anything else. He's always sailing his boat towards becoming the best he can be. Devote your energy and time in improving yourself for yourself, not for others.

## 10. Self-Belief Is Key

Rosanna once asked Lewis, "Is there ever a time when you doubt your own abilities?" "No," Lewis said. Without delving too deeply into this, it's a given that you should believe in yourself in the same way Hamilton does.

## Conclusion

Lewis Hamilton relentless determination towards being the best is what keeps him a champion. And just like him, always work towards perfecting what you are good at.

# PART 3

# Chapter 1:

## 10 Habits For A Clean Home

A clean home can make the homeowner a lot happier, less stressed, and even calmer. Waking up or coming back to a clutter-free and organized home can instantly brighten our mornings or even lift up our moods. But the thought of having to clean it extensively on weekends, for long hours, only to find the space in an absolute mess by midweek is like a nightmare and crestfallen.

Trust me when I say it is not that difficult maintaining a clean home. You need not necessarily have to deep clean your house almost every weekend for hours if you incorporate few very habits in your everyday routines. Today, we are exactly going to talk on this topic and hope to enlighten you to create a clean space.

Here are ten habits for a clean and happy home:

### 1. Make Your Bed As Soon as You Wake Up

We have heard a million times that the first thing that we should do after waking up is to make our beds, but how many of us incorporate this habit daily? An unmade bed can pull down the overall appearance of your bedroom by making it look messy. So take few moments and tuck those sheets and put your pillows in order. Change your bed sheets or duvet covers, and pillow covers as and when necessary.

Making our beds clean our most comfortable and visible area in the house and gives a sense of achievement helps us stay motivated and in a fresh state of mind throughout the day. If tucking in bed sheets daily is too annoying for you simply switch to duvet covers; that might save you from some hassle.

### 2. Put Things Back in Place After Using Them

Almost every home has this one chair or one spot that is cluttered with clothes and random knick-knacks, and this area hardly gets cleaned. Moreover, it is a normal human tendency to go on to dump more and more pieces of stuff and increase the pile size.

The idea behind creating this pile is that you will put away all the things in one go in a single day, but who are we kidding? As the pile starts increasing, we start pushing away the task of keeping the things back in their original place. The best way to avoid creating clutter is to put things back in their true place as soon as their job is done.

I completely understand that after finishing a task, we never feel like getting up to put them back in their home and hinder the task until we feel like doing so. But if you can consciously put this little effort into not letting things sit on the ground or in random places and put them back as soon as their job is done for the day, it is going to save a lot of time and help you have a clean space.

This is also applicable to your freshly washed clothes. As soon as you have them cleaned, fold them and put them in the drawer where it belongs. This will save you the headache of doing so on a Saturday morning which can then be used for reading your favorite book.

## 3. Take Your Mess With You as You Leave the Room

This is another essential practice that can bring a huge difference in your life and your home if turned into a habit. The idea here is to try not to leave a room empty-handed. What does this mean?
Let us take an example to understand this. Suppose you are in your living room and are going to the kitchen to drink water. Before you leave the living room, scan the room and look if any dirty bowl or plate is sitting in the room that needs to go to the kitchen. Take that cutlery along with you and keep them in the sink or dishwasher.

After making this a habit, you can then start following the one-touch rule that states that you touch a used item only once! That means if you are taking out the trash, make sure to dump or dispose of it properly and not just take it out and keep it somewhere on the porch or garden as this will kill the whole idea behind the habit. If you are moving something, it is better that you keep them where they belong, else, leave them be.

## 4.  Have a House Cleaning Schedule

Maintain cleaning schedules like morning cleaning routines or weekly cleaning routines. This is basically distributing the cleaning of the entire house over an entire week rather than keeping the task to get done in a single day. Fix days for achieving a particular task, like on Wednesdays you can vacuum the living room and the bedroom and on Thursdays clean the other rooms and so on.

Make sure to assign 15 to 20 minutes each morning that you will strictly use for cleaning purposes. This will surely bring about a very positive impact on your house, and you will be in awe of how much cleaning can be done in those mere 15 - 20 minutes. Try to vacuum the hallways, entries, and all other high traffic regions of your home (including the kitchen) as frequently as possible as they tend to get dusty easily.

## 5.  Maintain a Laundry Routine

Maintain a proper laundry routine depending on whether you live alone or in a family. As the pile of clothes grows enough to go into the washing, do the needful immediately. Do not delay the task endlessly as remember it is always easier to wash one load of clothing at a day rather than washing multiple loads of cloth in a day.

If you live with a family, do laundry every alternate day and if you live alone, then make sure to do your laundry every weekend. Also, make it a habit of putting the dirty clothes in the basket immediately after changing out of it rather than keeping them at random places to wash them later.

## 6. Keep Your Shoes, Coats, and Umbrellas in Their Right Place

Make it a habit to open your shoes near the entrance, put them away properly, and not randomly throw them. Keep a basket near the entryway where you can store all the umbrellas. If possible, put up a key holder on the door to keep the car keys and door keys in an organized manner.

The same goes for your long coats. Do not just dump them anywhere right after returning home! Have hooks hidden behind the entry door or have a sleek cupboard near the exit to store the trenchcoats and the long coats away from sight. These little changes will instantly clean up space.

## 7. Relax Only After Finishing Your Chores

If you have a chore that requires immediate attention, do it! Do not sit and relax, as this will go on to delay the chore indefinitely, and you may even forget to do it. So get your chores done first, then sit and watch Netflix. Detain your tasks only when you are exhausted and desperately need a break.

## 8. Clean After Every Meal

Right after fishing your meal, clean up the place. I know what most of you are thinking, but trust me, relaxing after cleaning everything up will give you more satisfaction and help you have a cleaner home for sure. After having your lunch or dinner, keep all the plates in the washer and make sure to also clean the utensils that you used for cooking.

Clean the countertops, the burners, and also the table that you sat and ate on. Cleaning the countertops and tables immediately will save your furniture from an ugly stain and help you save a lot of energy and time you might have had to put in if you try to clean the spill the later day.

## 9. Clean Your Dishes and Sink Every Night

I wanted to say have a nighttime cleaning routine every day where you clean all the dishes from dinner or any other remaining dishes of the day, the sink, and the kitchen by placing all the ingredient containers in their rightful places. The nighttime routine would also include setting your dining table, setting the cushions on your sofa, and clearing out your fridge so that you have a clean and spacious fridge before you unpack your groceries.

But I understand that not many of us have the energy after a hectic day at work, so instead of doing the entire routine, just make sure to wash all the dishes and clean the sink thoroughly so that you wake up to a beautiful kitchen in the morning. I mean, who wants to wake up to a pile of dishes, right? Just give some extra time at night to clean out the kitchen to have a fresh start in the morning.

## 10. Get Rid Of Unnecessary Things

To have a clutter-free space, each item in your home must have a home of its own. For example, if you do not have a place to hang your towels, they will likely be lying here and there and making the space look messy. Thus, make sure each item has its own place to sleep. If you see there are free-flowing items, then it is time to declutter!

You do not need much space, but you definitely need fewer items that fit in the available space and are easier to manage. More items require more time to clean and put things away properly. Thus, it is easier and requires less time to clean a room with lesser items out on the floor or on the countertop. Hence, make it a habit of getting rid of all the unnecessary items. You can donate the items or gift them to your neighbors or friends. Recycle all the old newspaper and magazines as papers too contribute a lot to the messiness of any room.

**Extra Tip**: Always try to keep your cleaning supplies in easily visible and accessible areas. This will save you a lot of time and motivate you to clean up anything that should be done as soon as possible.

Be satisfied with clean enough! A home can neither be squeaky clean every day nor can it be cleaned in one day. It is a gradual process that requires a conscious effort being made daily.

A clean home can be easily achieved by following these tips and manifesting these practices as your daily habits.

# Chapter 2:

# Happy People Are Busy but Not Rushed

[Dan Pink](#) points to an [interesting new research finding](#) — the happiest people are those that are very busy but don't feel rushed:

**Who among us are the happiest? Newly published research suggests that fortunate folks have little or no excess time and yet seldom feel rushed.**

This clicks with me. I love blogging, but I hate being under time pressure to get it done. This tension is very nicely demonstrated in a recent study by [Hsee et al. (2010)](#). When given a choice, participants preferred to do nothing unless given the tiniest possible reason to do something: a piece of candy. Then they sprang into action.

**Not only did people only need the smallest inducement to keep busy, but they were also happier when doing something rather than nothing. It's as if people understand that being busy will keep them happier, but they need an excuse of some kind.**

Having plenty of time gives you a feeling of control. Anything that increases your *perception of control* over a situation (whether it increases your control or not) can substantially decrease your stress level.

In Colorado, Steve Maier at the University of Boulder says that the degree of control that organisms can exert over something that creates stress determines whether the stressor alters the organism's functioning. His findings indicate that only uncontrollable stressors cause harmful effects. Inescapable or uncontrollable stress can be destructive, whereas the same stress that feels escapable is less destructive, significantly so… **Over and over, scientists see that the perception of control over a stressor alters the stressor's impact.**

But heavy time pressure stresses you out and kills creativity. Low-to-moderate time pressure produces the best results.

**If managers regularly set impossibly short time-frames or impossibly high workloads, employees become stressed, unhappy, and unmotivated—burned out. Yet, people hate being bored. It was rare for any participant in our study to report a day with very low time pressure, such days—when they did occur—were also not conducive to positive inner work life. In general, low-to-moderate time pressure seems optimal for sustaining positive thoughts, feelings, and drives.**

Your reaction to being too busy and under time pressure might be to want to do nothing. But that can drop you into the bottom left corner. And this makes you more unhappy than anything:

…**surveys "continue to show the least happy group to be those who quite often have excess time." Boredom, it seems, is burdensome.**

So, stay busy—set goals. Challenge yourself, but make sure you have plenty of time to feel in control of the situation.

This is how games feel. And games are fun.

# Chapter 3:

# *Five Habits We Consider*

# *Harmless*

Familiarity breeds contempt. There are habits that we have become so accustomed to that hinder us from achieving our full potential. We consider them little and insignificant in our lives. Sometimes, we go to the extremes of defending ourselves when we are corrected and advised to abandon them. It is a sad state to be in and one that requires enlightenment and self-awareness to be able to get out of that quagmire. Here are five habits that we consider harmless:

### 1. Blue Screen Addiction

Blue screen addiction is the addiction to digital media and video games. This is a common problem, especially for millennials. It is often considered inconsequential, a myth that has been debunked by real-life experiences.

Most people spend a lot of time working through their computers, using their mobile phones or tablets, playing video games, or watching television. The use of digital media in this era is almost unavoidable. Regardless of this digital evolution, there have been some excesses. Heavy use of these devices has broken the social code since most people can only communicate through communication apps and not physically.

Faceless cyberbullies have attacked and trolled innocent netizens and ruined their reputation.

News spread fast via the internet and it is not a surprise that addiction to blue screens is on the rise. It is not as harmless as it may seem and its effects are long-lasting. It causes poor eyesight and sometimes migraines.

## 2. Procrastination

It is the habit of postponing tasks to be done presently to a later time. Most people relate to this habit that has grown roots in our lifestyle. Before you judge yourself harshly for doing this, statistics have it that over 80% of college students engage in procrastination and it has chronically affected at least 20% of adults. That is just the tip of the iceberg.

We comfort ourselves that we are not alone in this ocean that has drowned the ambitions and potential of many people. We err in finding comfort in this well-dressed misery of procrastination. It is not as harmless as it superficially looks.

Procrastination encourages laziness which has, in turn, made many people pay a higher price for engaging in it. Some have lost their employment for leaving incomplete tasks at work, others have missed out on promotions for incompetence and a further group has failed to secure business opportunities that required their attention at the opportune time when they had put everything on hold. What is the cost we are ready to pay for in procrastination?

We should sober up and abandon procrastination by acting on matters that need our immediate attention. Shelving our response for a later time causes more harm than good.

### 3. Making Obnoxious Jokes

There is a limit to the extreme one can go when making jokes. It should never go overboard to hurt the feelings of our friends and associates. Many times we underestimate or maybe do not consider the impact our words may have on our friends and those around us. We unknowingly hurt their self-esteem and they feel worthless after what turns out to be a bad joke. We should always know when to stop and apologize for our excesses because we never know how much we have hurt our friends when we make bad jokes about them.

It is inconsiderate of us not to take into account the struggles of our friends when we make fun of their situation. It seems harmless but has the potential to completely cut off one's dreams.

### 4. Building A Fortress

The single greatest mistake that we unknowingly commit is building a fortress for ourselves to hide from the rest of the world. Indeed, the world can sometimes be cruel and unforgiving, making us run to the nearest point of safety. We build walls instead of bridges to separate us from the harsh reality. This solution is short-lived because the fortress will cut you off from the rest of the world.

You will live in solitude without any news and over time your resources will be depleted. The fortress may not necessarily be physical but also social. As much as introverts manage to keep off squabbles and fights, they lack a network to connect. It is not safe to be alone in this ever-changing world. Find a person or group with whom you share common interests and build a network.

Your       network       is       your       net       worth.

### 5.  Glossing Over Facts

Facts should be the language you speak. We often omit or ignore facts that we deem irrelevant to us but surprisingly turn out to be very important. When you get your facts right, everything falls into place. Often, the average person does not go into the details. Remember the devil lies in the details? It is therein where you will find solutions to matters that you overlooked.

Stand out by grasping correct facts about a matter before you indulge in them. It is harmful not to be aware of your surroundings or get your facts right because it puts your competence on the relevant subject matter in question.

You should check out these five habits that we mistakenly consider harmless and adjust your approach.

# Chapter 4:

## 8 Habits That Can Make You Happy

We're always striving for something, whether it's a promotion, a new truck, or anything else. This brings us to an assumption that "when this happens, You'll finally be happy."

While these important events ultimately make us happy, research suggests that this pleasure does not last. A Northwestern University study compared the happiness levels of ordinary people to those who had won the massive lottery in the previous years. It was found that the happiness scores of both groups were nearly equal.

The false belief that significant life events determine your happiness or sorrow is so widespread that psychologists have given it a name- "impact bias." The truth is that event-based happiness is transitory. Satisfaction is artificial; either create it or not. Long-term happiness is achieved through several habits. Happy people develop behaviors that keep them satisfied daily.

Here are eight habits that can make you happy.

## 1. Take Pride in Life's Little Pleasures.

We are prone to falling into routines by nature. This is, in some ways, a positive thing. It helps conserve brainpower while also providing comfort. However, it is possible to be so engrossed in your routine that you neglect to enjoy the little pleasures in life. Happy people understand the value of savoring the taste of their meal, revel in a great discussion they just had, or even simply stepping outside to take a big breath of fresh air.

## 2. Make Efforts To Be Happy.

Nobody, not even the most ecstatically happy people, wakes up every day feeling this way. They work harder than everyone else. They understand how easy it is to fall into a routine where you don't check your emotions or actively strive to be happy and optimistic. People who are happy continually assess their moods and make decisions with their happiness in mind.

## 3. Help other people.

Helping others not only makes them happy, but it also makes you happy. Helping others creates a surge of dopamine, oxytocin, and serotonin, all of which generate pleasant sensations. According to Harvard research, people who assist others are ten times more likely to be focused at work and 40% more likely to be promoted. According to the same study, individuals who constantly provide social support are the most likely to be happy during stressful situations. As long as you don't overcommit yourself, helping others will positively affect your mood.

## 4. Have Deep Conversations.

Happy people understand that happiness and substance go hand in hand. They avoid gossip, trivial conversation, and passing judgment on others. Instead, they emphasize meaningful interactions. You should interact with others on a deeper level because it makes you feel good, creates emotional connections, and, importantly, it's an intriguing way to learn.

### 5. Get Enough Sleep.

I've pounded this one too hard over the years, and I can't emphasize enough how important sleep is for enhancing your attitude, focus, and self-control. When you sleep, your brain recharges, removing harmful proteins that accumulate as byproducts of regular neuronal activity during the day. This guarantees that you awaken alert and focused. When you don't get enough quality sleep, your energy, attention, and memory all suffer. Even in the absence of a stressor, sleep loss elevates stress hormone levels. Sleep is vital to happy individuals because it makes them feel good, and they know how bad they feel when they don't get enough sleep.

## 6. Surround yourself with the right people

Happiness is contagious; it spreads through people. Surrounding yourself with happy people boosts your confidence, encourages your creativity, and is simply enjoyable. Spending time with negative people has the opposite effect. They get others to join their self-pity party so that they may feel better about themselves. Consider this: if someone was smoking, would you sit there all afternoon inhaling the second-hand smoke? You'd step back, and you should do the same with negative people.

## 7. Always Stay Positive.

Everyone, even happy people, encounters difficulties daily. Instead of moaning about how things could or should have been, happy people think about what they are grateful for. Then they find the best approach to the situation, that is, dealing with it and moving on. Pessimism is a powerful source of sadness. Aside from the damaging effects on your mood, the problem with a pessimistic mindset is that it becomes a self-fulfilling prophecy. If you expect bad things, you are more likely to encounter horrific events. Gloomy thoughts are difficult to overcome unless you see how illogical they are. If you force yourself to look at the facts, you'll discover that things aren't nearly as awful as you think.

## 8. Maintain a Growth Mindset.

People's core attitudes can be classified into two types: fixed mindsets and growth mindsets. You believe you are who you are and cannot change if you have a fixed attitude. When you are challenged, this causes problems because anything that looks to be more than you can handle will make you feel despondent and overwhelmed. People with a growth mindset believe that with effort, they can progress. They are happy as a result of their improved ability to deal with adversity. They also outperform those with a fixed perspective because they welcome difficulties and see them as chances to learn something new.

## Conclusion

It can be tough to maintain happiness, but investing your energy in good habits will pay off. Adopting even a couple of the habits on this list will have a significant impact on your mood.

# Chapter 5:

## 10 Habits of Warren Buffet

Warren Buffett, popularly known as the "Oracle of Omaha", is the chairman and CEO of Berkshire Hathaway and an American investor, corporate magnate, and philanthropist. He's undoubtedly a well-known investor of all time-if, not history, continuously setting records of knowledge, talent, and a strong drive to reach his future objectives. Buffett is also a supporter of leadership and personal growth, and he shares his wealth of advice to help you better your decisions.

So, how did he land to success? Here are ten warren's habits, which would you benefits later on.

### 1. His Reading Habit

Reading- a habit that he adheres to religiously, is one rule that Warren Buffett considers key to success. So he reads The Wall Street Journal, USA Today, and Forbes in the mornings and The Financial Times, The New York Times, Omaha World-Herald, and American Banker throughout the day.

Reading is basic to improving your understanding. Among other books, self-improvement books are popular with Buffet. That's said, consider jogging your memory with a mind-stimulating activity like reading. Engage in "500" pages book, article, newspaper each day, in the area that self-improves your interests. Reading makes you more knowledgeable than other people.

## 2. Compound Your Life and Finances

As per Albert Einstein, "Compound interest is the world's eighth wonder." if you understand it, you earn it; if not, you pay it." Warren Buffet's approach to investments never changes. He maintains his compounding investment principle as an investing strategy and aligns it with thinking patterns.

Compounding is the practice of reinvesting your earnings in your principal to generate an exponential return. Are you compounding your life finances, relationships, reading? That is how knowledge operates. It accumulates in the same way that compound interest does. You can accomplish it, but best when you're determined!

## 3. Isolation Power

Despite becoming the world's best investor and stock market trader, Warren Buffett claims that living away from Wall Street helped him. When you block the outside influence, you think quickly, distract unimportant variables and the general din.

Isolation exposes you to more prospects as it keeps you from external influence and information, making you unique and infamous.

## 4. Managing Your Time Wisely

You'll have 24 hours a day, or 1,440 minutes. All the leaders and successful people like Warren have one thing in common because of how powerful it is: Time management.

### 5. Do What You Enjoy

Your career or business may start with low returns but approaching it in Warren's way means switching your mind entirely to the job. If your mind likes something and you feed it to it regularly, it never turns off.

Working for a low salary is a momentary inconvenience, but it multiplies at the rate your skills increases, and they grow tremendously because you enjoy doing it.

### 6. Inner and Outer Scorecards

The key question about how people act is whether they have an Internal or an outward scorecard. So, naturally, it is preferable to be happy with your Inner Score to live a peaceful and happy life.

Having an inner scorecard is being contented with your thoughts and making decisions based on those thoughts while ignoring external influences or judgement skills. The deal is to live through values that matter to you, especially when making tough financial decisions.

### 7. Mimic the Finest Managers' Leadership Behaviours

Much of your life endeavours are, in most cases, shaped by the person who you choose to admire and emulate. Warren's admiration of Tom Murphy scourged him to greatness in leading his businesses to success.

### 8. Understand What You Have

Know and understand the companies in which you have a stake. Examine and analyze what is going on within the company, not what is going on in the marketplace.

The company's operations should be straightforward such that you can explain to an 8-year-old child how the company produces money in one phase. Familiarize enough with your investments while keeping a tab with its exact worth.

## 9. Invest in Your Well-Being

The basic right towards success is your well-being. Take care of your mental and physical health first, especially when you're young. The importance of life's fundamentals- nutritious diet, regular exercise, and restful sleep-is self-evident. It all boils down to whether you're doing them correctly.

## 10. Create a Positive Reputation

Buffett's reputation stems from his moral and level-headed attitude to both his personal and business life. You should view your business/career as a reflection of yourself, which means you should be careful and sensitive of how your decisions influence others.

## Conclusion

Just as Warren, enhance your cognitive skills through learning to become more knowledgeable for bettering your life initiatives. While focusing on your major goals, take care of your mental and physical well-being.

Therefore, invest your efforts and time carefully because the returns will multiply eventually.

# Chapter 6:

## 8 Habits You Should Have For Life

The key to being happy, feeling energized, and having a productive life relies on a cycle of good habits. Achieving a state of spiritual and physical satisfaction is a conscious choice that you can make for yourself. Realize what attaining the greatest happiness means for you and strive to be as productive as you can to achieve that happiness. Work towards a sense of self-realization and start reaching for your goals one step at a time. Accomplishing this requires you to be confident and have a sense of self, built entirely on good habits. This includes having good attitudes, thoughts, and decision-making skills. Quoting the all-time favorite Poet-Maya Angelou, "a good life is achieved by liking who you are, what you do, and how you do it."

How do you put this in place? Living by good habits and discipline nourishes your potential and make you a better person in your surroundings.

Here are 8 habits you should adopt for life:

## 1. Create a clear Morning Routine That Is Non-Negotiable.

Creating a morning routine that you like and living up to it is essential. Before you start your day, you can turn to what you like doing be it running, meditating, or having a peaceful meal-time at breakfast. Whatever activities you choose based on your liking, kick start your day with that habit. Managing your morning routine and making it a habit enables you to start your day on a proactive and positive note. This will also help you in enhancing your mental health and productivity. Through trial and error find out what works best for you and stick to you day in and out.

## 2. Make a Point of Physically Exercising Your Body Muscles.

To jog your cognitive skills, relieve stress that has a hold on your performance stamina means that you need to exercise-go to the gym regularly or as much as you can. Do you still need more convincing reasons for hitting the gym? Here you go! Physical exercises increase your 'happy' moods chemically and propels the release of hormone endorphins. This hormone aids in getting rid of all the body and mind anxious feelings, hence enabling you to calm down.

## 3. Develop Quality Personal Relationships With Loved Ones.

The Harvard study of adult development has found that most of the existing long-term happiness for an individual is predicted through healthy relationships. Developing and maintaining close relationships with your loved ones or those close to people you consider family has been found to help someone live a longer and quality life. Hence it is the connections within your surroundings that make your life worthwhile.

4. Master an Attitude of Listening.

If you want to cultivate relationships in your life, be it professional or personal, communication is key. While communicating with your peers, family, or colleagues, you need to understand that listening to what they are saying is important. This is because you cannot have effective communication if it's one-sided. Remember that it is always important to value what others have to say. Their perspective might impact you, but most importantly, when you listen, you make others feel valued. Always try to understand the other party's point of view even if it defers from yours. Be open-minded to differing opinions. The more you listen, the more you get to learn.

➢ 5. Choose Natural Food Rather Than Processed Ones To Help Keep Your Brain Intact.

Whatever we eat always impacts our health, energy, moods, and concentration level. Whether you have weight issues or not, eating a healthy diet is essential. First off, the normality of having a healthy breakfast, lunch, or dinner is an act of practicing self-esteem and self-love. Therefore, eating healthy will always boost your self-esteem, lessen emotional issues, and your daily productivity will eventually be taken care of. If you choose to put unhealthy food in your body, you are not protecting the sanctuary that is giving you life. Make a conscious effort tot choose foods that give you the best chance of success, health, and wellness. As we all know, money can't buy health.

## 6. Be Appreciative More Than You Are Disparaging

Mastering the art of gratitude is a great way to live a happy, stress-free, healthy, and fulfilling life. As French writer Alphonse said: "We can complain because rose plants have thorns or we can rejoice as thorns also have roses." It's always easy to forget how fortunate you are while trying to push through life and the obstacles that come along with it. How do you master this art? Start a journal of appreciation to be grateful for the things you have. Take the time to appreciate those closest to you, those who care about you, and remember at least one good thing about yourself each and every day. Don't forget to make a note of what you have accomplished as well before you go to bed. The more you take notice of the little joys in life, the happier you will be.

## 7. Be With a Circle of Friends That Are Positive Minded.

Be careful about who you spend your precious time and energy with. A happy life can be contagious if we know where to attract it. Coincidentally, happiness is also the easiest way to develop positivity in our lives. With that in mind, choose to surround yourself which such people who will bring light into your world. Spend time with those who will nurture you each step of the way and don't hesitate to let go of the people who are eating away at your energy and spirits. Let's not forget the wise words of entrepreneur Jim Rohn, "You are the five people you spent the most time averagely. You only live once! Let it be worthwhile.

# 8. Take Breaks Regularly To Invest in Self-Care.

Although you might be very passionate about your work and your daily schedules, it is okay to take some time - an hour, minute, second, or even a day off. If you take a while to unwind, you will do wonderful things for your mood, mind, and self-esteem. Spend some time doing at least one thing that makes you feel good every day – whether it be listening to music, engaging in sports, starting a new hobby, dabbling in the arts, or even simply preparing a pleasant meal for yourself, you deserve to do it. Whatever floats your boat, don't neglect it!

Conclusion

Determination, persistence, and continuous effort are essential for the development of these habits. It can take just a few weeks or maybe more than a year to develop your habits, so long as you don't stop. It does not matter how long it takes.

What are you waiting for? Pull up your socks; it's your time to win at life.

# Chapter 7:

# *Five Habits That Make You Age Faster*

We will all get old one day. A day is coming when we will not have the youthful energy we presently enjoy. Everyone desires that this day should never come or rather come very late in our lifetime. Nevertheless, it is an inevitable occurrence. We can only delay it.

Here are five habits that make you age faster:

### 1. Unforgiveness

Unforgiveness is like hiding fire expecting that no one will notice. Eventually, the smoke will give you away. It arises when one deeply wrongs us leaving a trail of hurt and agony that cannot easily be forgotten. The offended party will never forget what was committed against him/her. Anytime he/she sees the other person, the bad memory is re-kindled.

It is unhealthy to hold on to such bad memories. They cause mental and emotional trauma. They cause and affect your health. When your health is affected due to your unforgiveness, you bear full consequences and can only blame yourself. However subtle it may seem, unforgiveness is responsible for the fast aging of many people who harbor it.

The offender could probably have even forgotten about it and moved on with his/her life. The victim is the one who will be left bearing the brunt of the hurt. Stress will manifest on your face in the form of contortions making you appear aged than you are. Choose forgiveness always and you will lead a happier youthful life.

## 2.  Bitterness

Bitterness is an aftermath of unforgiveness. It is a very strong emotion that succeeds unforgiveness. Regardless that it springs forth from within, bitterness manifests on the face over time. The glory on the face of a joyous person is absent on that of a bitter person.

Ever asked yourself how people can judge someone's age bracket? The youthful glamour disappears on the face of a bitter person. Some elderly people appear very youthful. The reason is that they live a bitter-free life. Such a type of lifestyle guarantees youthfulness.

Strive to be youthful and live a fulfilling life by keeping bitterness at bay. Entertaining it will increase the rate at which you age and may succumb to old-age diseases while still at a very young age.

## 3.  Lack of Physical Exercise

Physical exercise is an important part of the human routine. It is not reserved for sports people only but everyone needs it to grow healthy. So important is exercise that it is incorporated in the education curriculum for students to observe.

Physical exercises help one become healthy and look youthful. It burns excess calories in our body and unblocks blood vessels thus increasing the efficiency of blood flow and body metabolism. Excess water, salts, and toxins are expelled from our bodies when we sweat after intense exercise.

The lack of physical exercise makes our bodies stiff and they become a fertile ground for lifestyle diseases like high blood pressure. Conversely, exercises improve our body shape and sizes by shedding extra weight. This healthy lifestyle brought by regular exercises will enable us to live a long healthy disease-free life.

## 4. Poor Dieting

Dieting serves several purposes but the chief benefit of a proper dieting habit is that it gives the body important nutrients and shields it from excesses caused by human bias. Proper dieting will make you eat nutritive food that you may even not like. The benefits of nutritive meals outweigh your tastes and preferences.

Poor dieting is taking meals without considering their nutritive value or repetitively eating a meal because you love it. This habit makes you caution less with what you eat. You will ingest excess oily and fatty foods which will harm the healthy bacteria that live in your gut. It goes further to affect your heart health and immune response to diseases.

These factors directly affect the rate at which you age. Greasy foods will manifest in your skin and alter your appearance. It may also cause acne on your face. To reduce your aging rate, improve your dieting habit and supply the body with the right nutrients.

## 5. Lack Of A Skincare Routine

As much as the skin is affected by the type of meals we take, a healthy skin care routine plays a major role in maintaining youthful skin. There are many celebrities globally who look younger than their age and this has a lot to do with their skincare routine.

It varies from one person to another but the fundamentals are constant - washing your face with plenty of clean water in the morning and evening. This is to remove dirt and dead cells from the skin. When one does not take care of his/her skin, aging creeps in. The face is the most visible part of the human body and it requires maximum care.

Failure to have an efficient skincare routine will entertain old age - the last item on our wish list.

Since we are now enlightened about habits that will make us age faster, the onus is on us to fight them and remain youthful.

# Chapter 8:

# _Five Habits That Can Make Someone Like You_

Favor and love are won. It is an endless race in life that requires zeal. You have to appeal to the other person so that they can like you back and return some affection. We often struggle to make those around us realize that we like them. Sometimes we succeed and at other times, we learn (not lose). The struggle is real and we need to measure up to the task.

Here are five habits that can make someone like you:

### 1.  Compliment Them Genuinely

Do not underestimate the power of a simple compliment on someone. A compliment is an indication that you recognize the other person's excellence in something. Appreciate their dressing, skills, effort or assistance lent to you by saying a 'thank you or you look amazing today!' When you make people feel loved by often genuinely complimenting them, they get motivated and feel loved. Always give genuine compliments and avoid faking them because it may come out as envy or jealousy. Instead of building bridges with the other person, you would have unknowingly built a wall.

Wouldn't you like someone who genuinely compliments you? Of course, you would. The glory that fills your heart when you are complimented will draw you to the other person. Genuine compliments are given in private or public. It is hypocritical to wait to be in public before you compliment someone. There is no occasion for acknowledging another. As long as it is in their presence, do not shy away from it.

## 2. Support Their Initiatives

Be in the front line to support the businesses and initiatives of those you want to court their attention. Be in their cheering squad and support their businesses and careers in whatever capacity. To be able to make someone like you, first court their attention, and what better way is there than to show up in those activities that matter to them?

If you develop the habit of being their ambassador in their businesses, they will see that you both have aligned goals and may take a keen interest in you. Their liking for you will grow as you appreciate their work and interests. Supporting their initiatives also means advising them on matters you are competent in. Your input should not be sycophancy but aimed at making a change.

Those you want to like you will do so in appreciation of your invaluable input in their work. Your ties will be stronger and they will like you more beyond your unconditional support. Be careful to maintain the relationship between you two. It is fragile more so that you are the one initiating it and it is up to them to fall for it.

## 3. Stand Up For Them

What can your friends say about you in your absence? This is a rare quality that most people look for when searching for potential friends or associates. If you want someone to like you, stand up for them in their absence. Your testimony about them to other people should be positive, one that will inspire their love for you.

You cannot possibly expect someone to like you if you speak negatively about them behind their back. Your words will haunt you should the one you intended for hears it. It should be something that you can confidently repeat to their face. Your sanctity will make you stand out when you stand up for your friends (pun intended).

Standing up for people you want to like you is a good way of 'shouting' your support for them. They will rush to see who it is that defended their character in public and will develop a special liking for you. Furthermore, you should do this in a manner that attracts respect and decorum to the one you are publicly defending.

## 4.   Be Dignified

You are what you attract. It begins with your attributes and how you carry yourself around. This plays a significant role in the perception of other people towards you. What is their opinion about you? Is it desirable enough to make them like you? Work on how you present yourself to other people and you will be irresistibly likable.

There is never a second chance to make a first impression. It is up to you to ensure that the first impression which sticks is the correct one. Carry yourself with dignity in everything you do because you never know who is watching. Random strangers will automatically like you as they observe your personal and public life.

## 5.  Be Humble

Humility is a rare virtue in most people. Nobody wants to be associated with violent friends because their rage makes them unpredictable. Humbleness does not mean you have allowed people to mistreat you. It means you are intelligent enough to choose your battles wisely.

Humble people are likable to a fault. People are attracted to calm personalities. They look mature, responsible, and chaos-free. Portray a positive image of yourself and you will be amazed at how people will like you.

Incorporating these five habits in your routine will make people like you and the icing of the cake is that whoever you aim to like you could be among them.

# Chapter 9:

# *Five Habits of A Joy-Filled Marriage*

The institution of marriage is one shrouded in mystery. One that is so deep that even married couples have a hard time adjusting to it. Numerous divorces are filled at courts of law albeit the fact that these weddings were full of pomp and color. Nevertheless, some marriages have withstood the test of time despite facing several challenges.

Here are five habits of a joy-filled marriage:

## 1. Open Communication

Communication is the master key to unlocking joy in marriage. A majority of unions that have been annulled were caused by a communication breakdown. What holds you from communicating with your marriage partner?

There is the fear of your better half being judgmental when you express your concerns. It ought not to be the case. You should be able to speak freely with your partner. The purpose of communication is to understand his/her expectations and let them know yours too. When this fails, conflicts are bound to arise.

Prevention is better than cure. It is wise to iron out any potential areas of conflict before they arise. Open communication is fearlessly talking to your partner about issues the moment they surface in your marriage. It is unhealthy to suppress any discontentment you may have. Use diplomacy - founded in communication - to unlock joy. A couple can talk to each other about their deepest desires and worst fears if there is healthy communication between them. One is capable of fulfilling his/her partner's wishes because they know them well.

## 2.   Selflessness

Marriage is a union where two adults become one. The two are supposed to take care of each other and see themselves through thick and thin. This is impossible if either the husband or wife is selfish.

Selflessness is putting the needs of your partner ahead of your own. Who does not love to be well-taken care of? Your partner too does. In showing love to him/her, joy blossoms. Joy is found when the couple is happy with each other. The essence of marriage is to have a partner with whom you will share your life selflessly.

Tranquility prevails in marriage when both parties see the effort that the other is investing in. It is a show of commitment towards the success of the marriage. Invite joy in your marriage by being selflessly committed to it. It sets a good example for your family. Your children will grow up into responsible adults with the right values from a young age. That is the beauty of marriage.

## 3.   Pursue Common Goals

Two cannot walk together unless they agree. A married couple should share a common vision for them to read from the same page as they build their home together. When a couple is divided, the marriage will collapse. Joy in marriage is attained when a couple pursues common goals. They become each other's best friend and confidant. Conflict arises when the couple cannot agree on what to do jointly and subsequently, joy becomes a mirage if they cannot work towards a common purpose. In place of joy, grief reigns.

The dream of every couple is to have a joy-filled marriage. This will remain an illusion if the couple does not commit to a common goal. Marriage is a work in progress; there is room to develop common goals to pursue as a couple. It is never late.

## 4.   Have Mutual Respect

Love forms a marriage but mutual respect holds it together. It is the glue that keeps a couple together in the eternal union. Joy is not guaranteed in marriage but is cultivated by the couple having mutual respect.

They will never insult each other in public or private. There is a golden rule in marriage - defend your partner in public but correct them in private. You should ensure that the public image of your partner is as clean as possible and always step up in areas of their deficiency. Anything that affects them directly touches you.

When your partner sees the concern you have for their image, they will return the respect which you have rightfully earned. This kind of relationship in marriage nurtures love and joy. Mutual respect will restrict you from making fun of or interfering with your partner's beliefs. These boundaries will be available when your relationship with your partner is healthy.

## 5.  Do Things Together

You must develop the habit of doing things together as a couple. This simple routine will make you bond more and get to understand your partner better. The blessings of an overflow of joy will be your portion in marriage.

When you do things together with your partner, it signifies your concern and love for each other because you do not want them to be overwhelmed. Moreover, you save time when you combine efforts.

These are the five habits of a joy-filled marriage. Incorporate them into your marriage and enjoy joy at its peak.

# Chapter 10:

# *Five Habits of Permanent Weight Loss*

Weight loss is a journey that many people have embarked on. Some of them are doing so out of personal ambition and others out of a doctor's advice. Regardless of their effort, somehow they seem not to be shedding off enough weight. Sometimes, even after losing a substantial amount of weight, they regain it once more and all their effort goes down the drain.

Here are five habits of permanent weight loss:

## 1. Win Both The Battle and The War

The mind is the arena of the greatest battle. Regardless that weight gain and loss manifests physically, the mind influences greatly on either outcome. When the battle is lost in the mind, the war against weight gain is subsequently lost.

Train your mind in a manner that suits you to be on the winning side. How so? A disciplined mind will win over your body to adhere to a strict routine geared towards weight loss. When you strengthen your mind not to succumb to temptations that will make you lapse in your weight loss journey, you have won half the battle.

As much as you put strategies in place to follow a particular routine, it is bound to fail if you have a weak mindset. No plan you put in place (that of weight loss included) will ever see the light of day when you are mentally unprepared. Similar to how one exercises body muscles, the brain too needs exercise. When your mind can withstand the temptations of eating anything, permanent weight loss is achievable.

## 2.  Seek Professional Help

The best way to solve a problem is to involve experts. Their insight will diagnose the heart of the problem and prescribe a lasting solution. The journey of weight loss gets easier when you follow the advice of medical doctors. You will know what to do not to cause harm to your body.

The ambition of permanent weight loss may get in your way and make you try wild things to achieve your goal. Some people go to the extent of taking herbal concoctions with the belief that it will help them shed some weight. There are instances where these concoctions have caused more harm than the good they intended.

Most people ignore the advice of doctors regarding weight loss. Instead, they prefer some weird prescription of homemade beverages with the hope of permanent weight loss. There is no shortcut to reaching your goal. When you seek professional help regarding how to adjust your lifestyle, you will not lapse back or add extra weight. Permanent weight loss is achievable.

## 3.  Associate With Like-Minded People

It is said that when you want to go fast, go alone but when you want to go far, go with someone. The journey of weight loss is long when you walk alone. Sometimes you may give up on the way and not achieve your goal.

In the company of people with whom you share a common goal – permanent weight loss –, you will encourage each other. In the small circle of friends, you will be able to exchange ideas and strategies for weight loss. This is unachievable when you isolate yourself.

The major challenge that may initially arise is finding the right group of people with whom you share a common goal. In the wrong group, you will be misplaced and permanent weight loss will forever remain a dream. Actualize this dream by excusing yourself from any rudderless group of people.

### 4. Lifestyle Change

A lifestyle change is a personal decision that one initiates without any external influence whatsoever. It is a conscious decision that one takes while being fully aware of the disruption it may have on his/her life.

Permanent weight loss is possible when one overhauls his/her lifestyle. When you stop taking alcohol or the habit of always driving even over short distances that you could walk, you will start shedding off some weight. Even an innocent habit of sleeping too much during the day will make you add some weight. Avoid it at all costs.

When you do a lifestyle audit and eliminate habits that will work against your goal of weight loss, the destination of permanent weight loss draws nearer. A lifestyle change is a difficult decision but one worth undertaking.

### 5. Seek Knowledge

Knowledge is power. Seek correct information on weight loss and avoid dwelling on myths, hearsay, and unfounded beliefs. Misinformation and misplacement of facts about weight loss will make it untenable. The fight against weight gain will have a big boost when there are sufficient facts about it.

The goal is not just weight loss but permanent weight loss. How is it achievable if we lack facts about it? Read and consult widely and approach it from a knowledgeable and informed point of view. Do not act blindly on fallacies.

These five habits for permanent weight loss bring significant change when adhered to.

# *Five Habits For A Beautiful Life*

A beautiful life means different things to different people. However, there are some things that we can all agree about. It is a happy one. Some of us have chased this kind of life but it has proven elusive to the brink of throwing in the towel. We play a greater role in designing a beautiful life for ourselves than others do in our lives.

Here are five habits for a beautiful life:

## 1. Live The Moment

This is not a call to carelessness. The focal point is to cherish the present moment. We are often distracted by our past experiences even in times when we ought to celebrate our current wins. The present is beautiful because we can influence it.

A beautiful life is joyous and the envy of those who cannot experience it. Savor the present completely and do not be entangled in the past. The past will withhold you from leveraging the opportunities popping up presently. Every saint has a past and every sinner has a future. You can shape the future by living in the moment and not dwelling in the past.

Worrying about the future is not beneficial. If you can change a situation, why worry? If you cannot also change anything, why worry? It is pointless to take the burden of occurrences that are yet to happen. Enjoy your present successes while you can and lead the beautiful life you have been dreaming of.

## 2.  Plan Wisely

Like everything invaluable, a beautiful life should be planned for. Planning is an integral part of determining whether a beautiful flawless life is achievable or not. It is not an event but a process that requires meticulous attention.

Planning entails extensive allocation of resources to life priorities. You should get your priorities right for things to run smoothly. In planning, your judgment and conscience should be as clear as a cloudless night. Any conflict of interest that could arise will jeopardize the attainment of a beautiful life - the ultimate goal.

We may be forced to make some painful sacrifices along the way and possibly give up short-time pleasures for long-term comfort. It may bring some discomfort but is worth the attainment of a beautiful life. Planning is a heavy price that must be made a routine to anyone aspiring to this magnificent dream.

## 3.  Pursue Your Purpose

Your purpose is the sole reason that keeps you going in life. You should pursue what motivates you to keep chasing your dreams. A beautiful life is one of fulfillment. Your purpose will bring it effortlessly if you remain loyal to it.

Focusing on your purpose can be a daunting task to an undisciplined mind. Many distractions may come up to make you stray or shift goalposts. You need to be disciplined to continue treading in the narrow path of your purpose. Do not lose sight of the antelope (a beautiful life) because of a dashing squirrel (distractions).

Living a life of purpose will satisfy you because you will willfully do what brings you joy; not what circumstances have forced you to. A cheerful way to live each day like it is your last is by finding pleasure in your routine activities and by extension, your purpose. Pursue it boldly!

## 4. Cut Your Coat According To Your Cloth

Live within your means and cut on unnecessary costs. Many people struggle to live within a particular social class that they are not able to afford at the moment. In the process of fitting in, they incur unmanageable debt.

A beautiful life does not mean one of luxury. It is stress-free and affordable within your space. It is unimaginable that one will wear himself/herself out to live a lifestyle beyond reach. Societal pressure should not push you to the brink of self-destruction as you try to fit in other people's shoes.

Even as you work towards your goals, do not suffocate yourself to please other people. Accept your financial status and make your budget within it. You will have an authentic and beautiful life.

## 5. Share Your Life With Your Loved Ones

We all have our families and loved ones. Our parents, siblings, spouses, and children should share our lives with us. It is beautiful and desirable that we intertwin our social and personal lives. The warmth and love of our families will put a smile on our faces despite any challenges.

Often, our families are the backbone of our emotional support. We retreat to them when we are wounded by the struggles of life and they nurse us back to health. Their presence and contribution to our lives are immeasurable. Family does not necessarily mean you have to be related by blood.

Some people are strong pillars in our lives and have seen us through hard times. Over time, they have become part of our family. We should share our lives with them and treasure each moment. We would be building a beautiful life for ourselves and the upcoming generations.

These are five habits we need to develop for a beautiful life. We only live once and should enjoy our lifetime by all means.

CPSIA information can be obtained
at www.ICGtesting.com
Printed in the USA
BVHW091945221221
624600BV00015B/1931